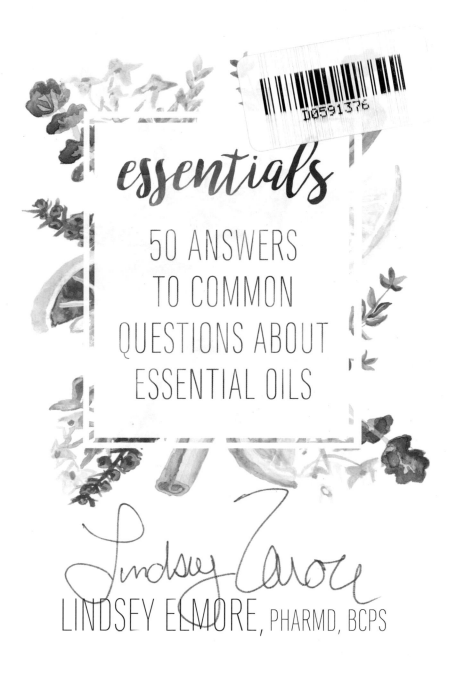

essentials

50 ANSWERS TO COMMON QUESTIONS ABOUT ESSENTIAL OILS

Lindsey Elmore

LINDSEY ELMORE, PHARMD, BCPS

growing
HEALTHY
HOMES

ISBN: 978-0-9988534-2-0
Printed in the United States of America
First printing.

Growing Healthy Homes LLC
P.O. Box 3154
Bartlesville, OK 74006

To obtain additional copies of this book, please visit
www.GrowingHealthyHomes.com.

Disclaimer: The information presented in the book is for educational purposes only. It is not intended to diagnose, treat, cure, or prevent any disease or illness. If you have a medical condition, please consult the health care provider of your choice.

The author is not liable for the misuse or misunderstanding of any information contained within this publication.

Quality, consistency and sustainability are important when it comes to choosing essential oils. The author only chooses Young Living Essential Oils for her home.

To Benjy, who empowers me to pursue the wildest
of dreams in ways I never thought possible.

TABLE OF CONTENTS

ADVANCED PRAISE 7

FOREWARD...8

INTRODUCTION 10

THE TEN BASICS

1. What are essential oils? 15
2. How can essential oils be used?........................17
3. Can essential oils *really* be safely ingested?.....21
4. What are the basics of essential oil chemistry?.....27
5. How are essential oils extracted from plants? 33
6. Do essential oils expire? 39
7. Do essential oils contain vitamins, proteins, or enzymes?...43
8. Do allergies to essential oils exist? 45
9. Where can I look for credible information about essential oils?...53
10. What are the best ways to travel with essential oils?...57

ESSENTIAL OIL CHEMISTRY AND PHYSIOLOGY

11. How do we perceive smells? 63
12. Can essential oil molecules enter the brain? 67
13. How do essential oils interact with bacteria?......71

ESSENTIAL OIL USAGE

14. Is there a best way to use an oil?.......................77
15. Where should I apply essential oils on my skin?.......81
16. How do I choose the best possible essential oil?.......85
17. Can essential oils be applied directly to the skin without dilution? 89
18. Are there optimal dilution ratios? 93

19. Can essential oils be instilled in the eye? 97
20. How do I choose the best diffuser? 99
21. Are there any precautions I should take
    before diffusing? 103
22. Does cooking or adding an essential oil in a
    beverage alter the chemical profile? 107

ESSENTIAL OIL REACTIONS
23. What are the essential oils that are most likely to
    cause skin irritation? 113
24. Why do some people get headaches after inhaling
    essential oils? 115
25. How quickly do essential oils enter the
    blood stream? 119
26. How do essential oils impact hormones? 123
27. What is the safest carrier oil for someone
    with nut allergies? 131
28. Can you develop a tolerance or immunity to
    essential oils? 135
29. If you are allergic to a plant, are you allergic to
    the essential oil of that same plant? 139

DISEASE STATE INTERACTIONS
30. Can essential oils be used in people with contact or
    allergic dermatitis? 145
31. Why is there a warning for basil essential oil for use
    in people with seizures? 149
32. Can people with diabetes use essential oils? 153
33. Can people with lung diseases use essential oils? 157
34. Should people with autoimmune diseases use
    essential oils? 167
35. Should peppermint essential oil be avoided in
    people with heartburn? 171
36. Can people with a history of estrogen-linked
    cancer use essential oils? 175

37. Can people with hypertension use essential oils? 179
38. Can people who have had a transplant use
     essential oils? 183

DRUG AND TESTING INTERACTIONS

39. What are drug interactions and where do
     they arise? 189
40. Does grapefruit essential oil interact with
     medications? 195
41. Do essential oils interact with blood thinners? 197
42. Do essential oils interact with birth control pills? 199
43. Can essential oils cause a false positive on a
     drug test? 203

SPECIAL POPULATIONS

44. What essential oils should I avoid if I am pregnant
     or nursing? 209
45. Are essential oils safe to use for children? 217
46. Does lavender oil cause breast swelling in
     young boys? 223
47. Can essential oils I use affect my children? 225

SPECIFIC ESSENTIAL OILS

48. I've read that tea tree essential oil is extremely
     dangerous. What are the real risks? 229
49. What are the differences in frankincense species? 233
50. What is the difference between species of
     lavender? 237

MORE ESSENTIALS 241

GLOSSARY 249

REFERENCES 252

ACKNOWLEDGEMENTS 285

BIOGRAPHY 286

INDEX 288

ADVANCED PRAISE

Dr. Lindsey Elmore has written a book to empower us all! With her beautiful images and her personable, educational explanations, Dr. Elmore puts our health back in our hands and leaves us confident about the next move by giving the reader the knowledge of essential oil safety and usage. Dr. Elmore leads you outside the box and into a new, refreshing view on health and wellness.

– Amber Myers, PharmD

For anyone with a goal to learn more about essential oils or grow a business, Dr. Lindsey Elmore's *Essentials* is a must read. This book makes even complicated science of essential oils easy to understand all presented in a beautifully crafted book.

– The Oola Guys

Are you baffled by the science of essential oils, but want to help your research-driven friends? As an RN and Aromatherapist, this book makes my geeky heart skip a beat! With so much amazing information you will be able to answer those tough questions, and you will want to share the book with everyone you know!

– Julie Folger, RN, BSN, CN

Dr. Lindsey Elmore is one of the best educators on all things physiology and especially essential oils. Having seen her in action and now reading her book, I can say she writes even better than she speaks! Great resource for both the scientific mind AND the person just needing basics.

– Jim Bob Haggerton, DC, CCWP

As a European Osteopath and Integrative Practitioner, it is essential to know how to combine natural products with Western approaches to health. I find Dr. Lindsey Elmore, a pharmacist and advocate of integrative medicine, an invaluable resource. This gorgeous book is a must have for everyone looking find total wellness!

– Vicky Vlachonis, European Osteopath & author of The Body Doesn't Lie

FOREWORD

Have you ever wished that you had all of the important answers to essential oils, but there is just so much to know? Like how can you use these magical essential oils? Can you use them topically, diffuse them, or can you actually ingest them or perhaps cook with them? Is it safe? Can I use essential oils on my children? Phenols, monoterpenes, sesquiterpenes... OH MY!?

There is so much to learn and understand about these essential oils, and Dr. Lindsey Elmore helps us to better understand in depth about these essential oils everybody is raving about. Maybe you want a short answer; maybe you're looking for a more detailed in-depth answer. Wouldn't it be great if you had a book that offered such things that you could access and have in your toolbox at any time? To have the knowledge and to be able to answer these questions when your friends, family, and co-workers ask you is a powerful thing. Well, look no further, THIS IS THE BOOK you are looking for and you will not want to be without it.

Dr. Lindsey Elmore is one of the most inspiring and motivational women I know. With an undergraduate degree in Chemistry and a doctorate in Pharmacy, Dr. Lindsey Elmore shares her wealth of knowledge with all of us in this book... Not to mention she is also a global product educator with Young Living Essential Oils. So yes, this girl knows what she's talking about!

Now, let's just add incredible author to her resume. She has the power to inspire and the ability to move people with her teachings. Her knowledge is evident in every word she speaks. Having the opportunity to watch her live Facebook classes each week is an absolute treat. Her love of whatever topic she is talking about shows; it beams from her face. When Lindsey speaks, I am engaged from start to finish, always wanting more.

This book was no different. For me, it was like taking an essential oils adventure – a really FUN, exciting, educational adventure. I couldn't set this book down because I kept wanting to know what was on each page. What was I going to learn next? I love how this book is broken down into no-nonsense and straight-forward facts, organized into SHORT answers and LONG answers. With that being said, you won't want to just read the short answer. Your brain automatically wants to learn more and you feel more confident as you know more about these essential oils. The charts/ graphs/ pictures included help you visually understand the breakdown of the oils. You really get a sense of her expertise and knowledge on the topic as she literally shines. I felt like I was actually in Lindsey's amazing brain.

If you are trying to Google all of the answers to the questions you may have about essential oils, this book is going to give you all the answers and bring you joy in the process. Not to mention, business builders, how it will catapult your business.

Dr. Lindsey Elmore does an exceptional job in helping all of us to believe in ourselves and these essential oils. I highly recommend that you read this book from cover to end. It is loaded with everything you ever wanted to know. You have a question? The answers are inside.

– *Jen Davis*

INTRODUCTION

Though this book makes suggestions on how to best use essential oils, it is not intended to be a doctrine or manifesto, nor is the advice the only way to use essential oils and natural products safely. The book is intended to offer common sense and evidence-based answers to some of the most common questions about essential oils and natural products. That is why I wrote this book: to empower others to address the most common questions that I encounter as I teach and share the power of essential oils with others. The amount of information out there about essential oils is almost infinite, and it is impossible to know it all. However for me, it is less important to know all the information, and it is much more important to know common sense safety, science, and usage information. Some answers will have similar information despite the questions being different. The reason for this is three-fold. First, repetition is a key to mastery. By repeating the same information several times in diverse contexts, I hope that you will be better equipped to grasp and later recall the information. Second, principles of essential oil chemistry and physiology relate to safety, usage, and interactions with drugs and disease states in similar ways; therefore, it is impossible not to overlap information. Third, this book is not necessarily intended to be read cover to cover in one sitting. Instead, utilize this book when questions come up, and you are unsure how to answer them.

Some of the answers in this book contain extensive references, and others do not. When there are references, I have relied on the cited author's publication to form my opinion. When there are few or no references, I have relied on my own personal experiences to form my opinion.

There are times when language in this book is simple and straight-forward. There are other times when language is more technical. If you do not know a word, please consult the glossary; hopefully I defined it there. If it is still unclear, please reach out to me, and we will figure it out together.

There is data in this book related to a wide variety of essential oils, some of which are widely available (like lavender), while others are not as widely available (like red cedar). There are also some that are not available from any direct to consumer supplier. For many of the oils, I list their primary chemical constituents. If you are unfamiliar with an essential oil or the chemical constituents, there are a wide variety of textbooks and reliable online articles that can detail the chemical breakdown of the essential oil. Once you know the chemical constituents, it can lead you to an alternative essential oil that is more readily accessible.

More than anything, enjoy reading, enjoy learning, and enjoy using essential oils. Let's get started with section one on the top ten questions I hear from new users of essential oils!

– Lindsey

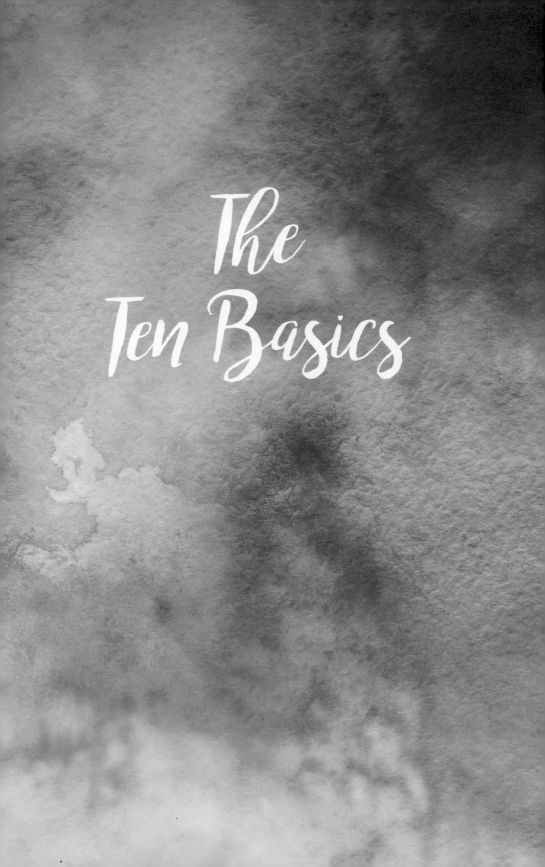

The Ten Basics

In this section, we will review some of the most basic questions about essential oils that every beginner should know.

#1
WHAT ARE ESSENTIAL OILS?

LAVENDER
Lavandula angustifolia

Short Answer

Essential oils are natural, aromatic oils typically obtained through the distillation of plant material.

Long Answer

Essential oils are natural, aromatic oils typically obtained through the distillation of plant material. Essential oils can be present in the leaves, flowers, stems, or roots, and they have the characteristic odor of the plant from which they were obtained. Distillation, resin tapping, cold-pressing, or absolute extraction concentrate the plant molecules while intensifying the aroma of the plant in the essential oil.

Inside the plant, essential oils act as protectors against fungi, bacteria, insects, and other predators, play an important role in attracting pollinators, and prevent other plants from growing in their territory. Humans have used essential oils for many centuries and across many cultures for their aromas and flavors to enhance wellness, spirituality, recipes, and cosmetic products.

Essential oils contain thousands of volatile compounds that evaporate quickly into the air, and the ratio of the molecules imparts the aroma to the oil. The season of the year, geography, and distillation techniques can change the ratio of the molecules resulting in subtle (or maybe dramatic) differences in the aroma, volatility (how quickly the essential evaporates into the air), and how the essential oil feels on the skin.

#2

HOW CAN ESSENTIAL OILS BE USED?

CEDARWOOD
Cedrus atlantica

Short Answer

Essential oils can be inhaled aromatically, applied topically to the skin, or ingested by mouth.

Long Answer

Essential oils can be inhaled aromatically, applied topically to the skin, or ingested by mouth. If you are unsure where to start, please note that every essential oil is labeled with instructions for use.

First, try aromatic use. If you have never used an essential oil, simply opening the bottle is an excellent place to start. Open the bottle, inhale, and enjoy. If you do not enjoy the aroma, you can try a different method (such as applying to the skin or adding to a recipe), or you can select another essential oil. Add a few drops of essential oil to a diffuser to transform the aroma (and potentially the mood) of an environment.

Next, try an essential oil topically on your skin. If you have never used an essential oil on your skin, you may choose to start by applying it on the bottoms of the feet or the palms of the hands. Some areas are more sensitive than others, and for first time users (and many experienced users), it is recommended to avoid overuse of essential oils under the arms, on the face or genitalia, on skin that is broken, or any other area of the body that you find sensitive.

Many people choose to use essential oils undiluted on the skin. If you choose to use the oil undiluted, be aware that some oils can be perceived as warm or hot on the skin, and others can be perceived as cold. If an essential oil is too hot or too cold on the skin, simply add a bit of a carrier oil. Carrier oils ensure that the application of essential oils is comfortable on the skin. You can use any natural, fatty oil you have around your home (almond, jojoba, coconut, olive, hemp, etc.) as a carrier oil. (Do not use petrolatum jelly, mineral oil, or any other synthetic oil.) If you choose to dilute an essential oil, take a bit of the carrier oil and blend it with the essential oil before applying to the skin. For the average adult, 1 drop of essential oil in 10 drops carrier oil is more than enough dilution to avoid any skin irritation, and in most cases less than that will be sufficient. This can be done in a small dish, in a roll-on container, or in your hand if you are simply worried about applying to sensitive skin or onto a young child.

Exercise caution when applying essential oils to the skin of very young children, especially premature infants. Some experts argue that essential oils should never be used on the skin of premature infants; however, many parents choose to use essential oils on very young infants after ensuring that the essential oil is heavily diluted in carrier oil (1 drop essential oil in 20, 50 even 100 or more drops of carrier oil). Use your best judgment as a parent to decide when it is right to introduce essential oil to your child's skin.

If you have very sensitive skin or if you want to exercise additional caution, consider a patch test procedure prior to first using an essential oil. To perform a patch test, apply 1-2 drops of essential oil to a patch of skin such as the forearm (you may opt to dilute the essential oil with a carrier oil before you apply). Observe that area of skin over the course of 1-2 hours for any noticeable reaction. If discomfort or irritation occurs, do not apply more essential oil, and apply carrier oil as often as needed to the affected area. Never use water to flush the oil off the skin, as this may increase discomfort. If you experience discomfort from an essential oil, dilute the essential oil before using again.

Essential oils may also be taken by mouth: directly dispensed on the tongue, placed in a capsule, or included in foods and beverages as a flavoring agents. In general, "start low and go

slow" as you begin to ingest essential oils. One to two drops
directly on the tongue or in a capsule can be enough to start.
When cooking with essential oils, a little bit goes a very long
way. Do not use more than is recommended in the recipe, as
the flavor of essential oils can be quite potent and can quickly
overpower a dish. Often, dipping a toothpick into the essential
oil and swirling in a batter, sauce, or beverage can be enough
to impart flavor to the dish.

There is no perfect time schedule to use an essential oil. Some
people choose to use essential oils very regularly – perhaps
3-4 times per day or more – while others only use as needed
for a specific reason or condition. Again, there is no one right
way to use essential oils, and it is up to you to decide how and
when you would like to use them. As you start, remember that
it does not take much essential oil to make a large difference to
the environment, to a food or beverage, or to your well-being
after inhalation or application on the skin. Excessive use (what
I loosely define throughout this text is using more than one
milliliter at one time, especially by mouth) is not recommended
unless you are experienced with essential oils and their effects
on your body.

#3

CAN ESSENTIAL OILS *REALLY* BE SAFELY INGESTED?

LEMON
Citrus limon

— *Short Answer* —

Yes, they can. You may wish to exercise caution not to overuse essential oils by mouth as they can cause gastrointestinal upset and can deplete glutathione.

Long Answer

Per the Food and Drug Administration, there are dozens of essential oils that are generally recognized as safe for ingestion (GRAS). This list includes resins not extracted by solvents, distillates, and cold pressed oils. Essential oils on the GRAS list include peppermint, cinnamon, clove, nutmeg, most citrus varieties, chamomile, geranium, and many more. Even some essential oils that are generally considered to contain constituents that have a greater risk than others such as hyssop, sage and mustard are included on the list.

EFFECTS ON TEETH

Lemon oils and other citrus oils are purported to damage the teeth, and the proportional damage is said to be linked to the concentration of citric acid. Citric acid is a weak acid that is water soluble and not contained within essential oils. In general, there are very few acids in essential oils, such as benzoic acid, cinnamic acid, and angelic acid; however, the concentration is low (<3%). While citrus juices, especially fresh lemon and lime juice, do contain a high concentration of citric acid (up to 8%), citric acid is not found within essential oils. In a private study, 55 milliliters of purified water was placed in a beaker, and the pH was measured at 4.7. Fifteen drops of orange essential oil were added to this beaker, and the pH did not change. An additional 10 drops of orange essential oil were added to the beaker, and the pH still did not change, indicating that little to no acids are contained in the oil. This was expected since acids are not oil soluble, and any acids that are removed from the plant during distillation remain in the aqueous phase of the distillate after separation. Conversely, an equal amount of freshly squeezed orange, lime, lemon, or tangerine juice caused the pH to shift downwards, representing a more than 10-fold increase of the solution's acidity. These results confirm that citrus essential oils do not contain the acids found in citrus juices and are very unlikely to cause acid erosion to enamel as a result.

Sugar is also well known to decay teeth by leaching calcium from the tooth, and studies have examined the ability of essential oils to inhibit the demineralization process. In an in vitro model, human teeth were soaked in 50 mL of apple juice and either sodium fluoride, clove essential oil, eugenol, or eugenyl acetate. Compared to the control group, which was apple juice alone, clove essential oil, eugenol, and eugenyl acetate reduced decalcification of the tooth to the same extent as the fluoride-treated tooth. Furthermore, fluoride was found to be significantly more cytotoxic than clove essential oil or its lead constituents.

LIVER EFFECTS

Ingestion of essential oils may get a bad reputation online for causing liver damage, especially when ingested over a long period of time. Studies have reported adverse reactions from depletion of metabolizing enzymes to death. Conversely, studies have also shown evidence of essential oils protecting the liver. The risk to the liver is directly linked to the metabolism of the essential oil constituents.

When essential oils are metabolized (the same as when other external compounds are metabolized), sometimes electrophiles are produced. Electrophiles are highly reactive molecules that require additional processing to in order to not become toxic. Any substance, in sufficient quantities, can overwhelm the liver and produce more electrophiles than the liver can metabolize, thus putting the liver at risk. Secondly, foreign substances, essential oils included, can potentially damage the liver by depleting glutathione. It's important to note that it takes a lot of essential oils to deplete glutathione, produce electrophiles, or cause liver damage. Studies suggest that 0.5 mL/kg of Cassia essential oil in rats can deplete glutathione. If that data is scaled up to a human, then it would take 35 mL just to begin the depletion process. There was a report that an 18-year old girl ingested 30 mL of pennyroyal essential oil and experienced massive hepatic necrosis; therefore, ingestion of excessive amounts of essential oil is not recommended.

The risk of ingesting large amounts of oil is also evident in two case reports of ingestion of 5-20 mL of clove essential oil in two children aged 15 months and 2 years, both of whom suffered liver damage as a result. In rats, large doses of menthol in soybean oil (equivalent to 15 mL/day) for 28 days caused vacuoles in the liver. Therefore, it is likely that damage to the liver is dependent upon the dose and that massive doses, especially massive doses over time, may cause damage.

On the other hand, certain essential oils, and some essential oil constituents, have protected against damage from foreign substances. Fennel and thyme oil protected against carbon tetrachloride damage, and garlic oil against acetaminophen (paracetamol) damage to the liver. Essential oils constituents such as thymoquinone can also induce glutathione and help the body eliminate toxins.

SUMMARY

When choosing to ingest or not ingest, it is important to cautiously interpret data and to pay special attention to the dose of the oil that is used in the study. The dose is often much higher than what would normally be ingested by a human. Side effects of ingesting essential oils are typically gastrointestinal. Some people experience belching (especially immediately after ingestion) and flatulence.

If you choose to use essential oils in water, the best containers for essential oils are ceramic, stainless steel, or glass, as they are less likely to react with essential oils than plastic.

#4

WHAT ARE THE BASICS OF ESSENTIAL OIL CHEMISTRY?

OREGANO
Origanum vulgarc

Short Answer

Essential oils contain a wide variety of molecules, and the most common ones are phenols, monoterpenes, and sesquiterpenes. In the plant, essential oils protect the plant from harm and help attract helpful pollinators.

Long Answer

Essential oils are naturally occurring, aromatic compounds that are found in the leaves, flowers, stems, roots and bark of plants. Essential oils are volatile and rise quickly into the air, bringing the aroma of the plant to the environment. Essential oils are distinctly different than fatty oils such as olive, almond, or coconut oils because they are small, compact, and non-greasy, whereas fatty oils are large, linear, and lubricating.

There are at least 13 different types of chemical compounds in essential oils including monoterpenes, sesquiterpenes, alcohols, esters, ethers, phenols, phenylpropanoids, aldehydes, ketones, oxides, lactones, and furanocoumarins. We will cover three of these compound types below in depth. These three compounds have an easy-to-remember acronym, 'PMS', which stands for Phenols, Monoterpenes, and Sesquiterpenes.

Terpenes, such as monoterpenes and sesquiterpenes, are built of isoprene units and are some of the most common chemicals in essential oils. Isoprene is the end-product of methyl-erythritol 4-phosphate (MEP) pathway metabolism, which takes place in the chloroplast in plants. The plant releases isoprene to combat stressors such as heat, free radicals, wind, drought, and floods. Isoprene also plays an important role in atmospheric science, helping to cool the planet. Isoprene is a very simple structure consisting of five carbons and eight hydrogens (Figure 1). Isoprene units combine in a wide variety of ways to form terpenes (also known as isoprenoids). Terpenes may contain as little as two isoprene units (monoterpenes) or as many as 1000+ units (such as natural rubber). The most common terpenes in essential oils are monoterpenes (Figure 2) and sesquiterpenes (Figure 3). Larger terpenes such as tri- and tetra-terpenes can be found in essential oils, but to a lesser extent than other terpenes. Mono- and sesquiterpenes are the smallest of the terpenes and have a molecular weight of less than 250 amu. Both mono- and sesquiterpenes interfere with cell proliferation and with immune processes. Certain terpenes can serve as phytoalexins and can repel deer, pests, and microbes away from plants. Sesquiterpene medications, such as artemisinin, have been used for their anti-inflammatory, anti-malarial, and antioxidant properties. Examples of monoterpenes include nerol, citral, camphor, and menthol, and examples of sesquiterpenes include nerolidol and farnesol. Because monoterpenes very readily react with oxygen in the air, it is important to keep essential oils high in monoterpenes (such as citrus oils) tightly closed or the essential oil is at risk for oxidation.

Essential oils also contain phenolic compounds. Phenols have a hydroxyl group directly attached to an aromatic ring (Figure 4). Phenols such as carvacrol are found in high levels in oregano essential oil, eugenol in clove, methyl salicylate in wintergreen, and thymol in thyme. In plants, phenols can act as protectors against herbivores, fungus, and bacteria and have psychoactive properties that further deter animal predators. There are a few medications that make use of the psychoactive properties of phenols to treat Parkinson's Disease or act as an anesthetic. The pleasant aroma of phenols can help to attract beneficial bacteria, pollinators, and animals that help disperse seeds. Because phenols must be metabolized by cytochromes, some experts contend that essential oils high in phenols should only be used intermittently instead of daily. If you choose to use essential oils high in phenols (such as basil, anise, clove, oregano, thyme, cinnamon, or cassia) by mouth, you may wish to use a bit less or use it only every few days. Most agree that essential oils high in phenols should be used with caution in animals that lack a cytochrome P450 system such as cats, reptiles, and birds, if used at all. Animals who lack a P450 system have a reduced ability to remove essential oil constituents from their bodies, and this can lead to potential side effects and levels above the healthy limit.

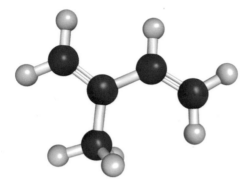

FIGURE 1. Isoprene structure consisting of five carbons and eight hydrogens.

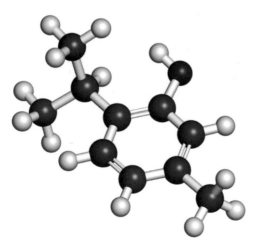

FIGURE 2. An example of Thymol (a monoterpene) with 10 carbons and 16 hydrogens.

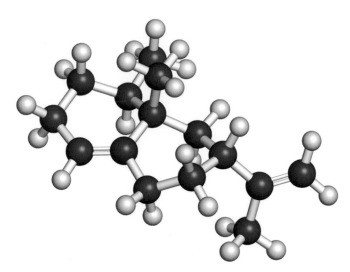

FIGURE 3. An example of Valencene (a sesquiterpene) with 15 carbons and 24 hydrogens.

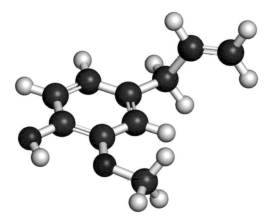

FIGURE 4. An example of Eugenol (a phenol) with a hydroxyl group directly beside an aromatic ring.

#5

HOW ARE ESSENTIAL OILS EXTRACTED FROM PLANTS?

BLACK SPRUCE
Picea mariana

Short Answer

Essential oils may be obtained through steam distillation, resin tapping, cold-pressing, or absolute extraction.

Long Answer

There are four basic ways that essential oils can be obtained from plants: distillation, resin tapping, cold-pressing and absolute extraction. Distillation is the most common way and is the preferred approach with most plants. Resin tapping is reserved for certain trees such as frankincense or copaiba that produce a thick sap. Cold-pressing is used primarily for citrus fruits. Absolute extraction is the rarest form of extraction, reserved for the most delicate of plants.

The distillation process begins with placing harvested plant material into a vat suspended over a water bath. As the water below plant material begins to boil, it generates steam that then percolates up through the plant material and catches essential oils on its way, generating a mixture of steam and oil. The mixture then flows down a condensing column where the essential oils are separated from the water. Imagine boiling a pot of water on your stove with a glass lid on top. As the steam rises and hits the glass lid, water droplets condense on the lid because the air outside the lid is colder than the water inside the pot. This same process happens repeatedly inside the condensing column, and because water and oil do not typically mix unless they are forced to, the essential oils separates naturally from the water when the water droplet hits the side of the cold condensing column. The newly separated mixture of water and oil flow to the collecting chamber, where water (aka hydrosol or floral water) settles at the bottom, and the naturally light essential oil flows to the top and can be collected. Steam distillation is the most common form of distillation and is used for a wide variety of plants including rosemary, basil, peppermint, thyme, cedarwood, and many more.

Resin tapping uses the steam distillation process as described above, but it adds in another step at the beginning. Before resin can be added to the vat suspended over steam, it must be collected from the trunk of a tree. To do this, multiple V-shaped cuts are made along the side of the trunk of the tree. The tree responds by secreting a protective resin (a bit like our bodies bleed and form a scab). This resin is then collected; in the case of frankincense it may be chewed directly out of the tree, burned in a resin burner, or steam distilled into essential oil. Resin tapping is only used for a select number of trees such as frankincense, copaiba, and other conifers. Just because a plant can be resin tapped does not mean that it will be to produce an essential oil; in the case of many conifers, the entire tree is steam distilled instead of just the resin.

Absolute extraction is the most complicated form of essential oil extraction because it requires repeated cycles of steam distillation, first with a solvent and then another extraction to remove the solvent from the essential oil. Simply, solvents are substances that dissolve other substances, and the most basic solvent is water.

In absolute extraction, the plant material and the solvent are first mixed together, and this extracts the essential oil from the plant, along with chlorophyll, waxes, and other plant tissue. This 'concrete' is rich in aromatic essential oils, but is still mixed with the solvent. Next the concrete is mixed with alcohol, which splits the essential oil from the solvent. The solvent is recycled back to the beginning of the process, and the aromatics are collected. There is a trace amount of solvent left behind in the process. Absolute extraction is used for plants that are very fragile and difficult to distill otherwise. Almost always, jasmine is an absolute essential oil, and, depending on the company, neroli, rose, mimosa, carnation, violet leaf, and more are as well.

The final way that essential oils can be extracted is via cold-pressing, also known as expression. Cold-pressing does not produce a true essential oil but an essence. In modern cold-pressing, the rinds of citrus fruits are hit with spikes, and the puncturing of the skin allows most of the essential oils to be expressed. Then, if you imagine a garlic press in your kitchen, the fruits are squeezed, releasing the juices and the essential oils that are then separated using centrifugal force. Cold-pressing can also be completed using only the rinds of fruits so that the juice does not have to be separated from the essential oil. Cold-pressing leaves behind trace amounts of waxes and residues in the process. It is used for plants that are very high in citral, and because citral burns very easily and lends a bitter aroma to the final essential oil, cold-pressing is the preferred method for extracting aromatic oils from citrus such as lemon, grapefruit, tangerine, bergamot, and lime.

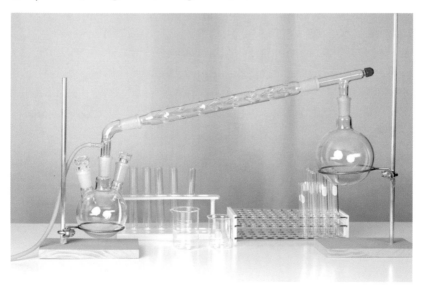

FIGURE 1: Steam distillation

FIGURE 2: Resin tapping

FIGURE 3: Cold-pressing

#6

DO ESSENTIAL OILS EXPIRE?

BLUE SPRUCE
Picea pungens

Short Answer

They do not expire exactly; they will not go putrid, grow mold, etc. However, they may oxidize, especially if not stored properly, and this can change the chemical profile.

Long Answer

Essential oils do not have a true expiration date. In fact, essential oils can remain stable for many years if they are stored in air-tight containers away from light and heat. When exposed to heat, light, or air, all essential oils can eventually break down. This can affect aroma, chemical constituents, efficacy, and lead to potential toxicity.

While essential oils have some tolerance to heat, sustained heat at or above approximately 80°F (28°C) over the course of days can cause significant damage. Essential oils are distilled at temperatures much higher than boiling, and they can withstand these temperatures and still maintain their aromatic qualities for a brief time. Upon exposure to sustained heat, essential oils show rapid breakdown of certain constituents including sabinene, 1,8-cineole, and linalool, whereas others do not seem to be as susceptible to heat, such as terpinen-4-ol and eugenol.

Essential oils such as citrus (grapefruit, lemon, bergamot, orange, etc.) and jasmine absolute are damaged quickly at temperatures greater than 90-100°F because they are expressed as absolute oils and not true essential oils. If these oils are above 90-100°F, you may consider allowing the oils to come back to room temperature before using them. If an essential oil smells like it has gone bad after exposure to heat, you may consider discarding the oil, as chemical degradation can affect the efficacy of an oil, and may generate new, hazardous compounds.

Cold temperatures will not generally harm any high quality essential oil, and studies show that cold temperatures can prevent oxidation. However, in oils that are thick or viscous, cold temperatures may make the oils too thick to pour from the bottle. If an essential oil is too thick, gently roll the bottle in between your palms to warm the essential oil, and this will encourage it to fall out of the bottle.

Oxygen can also break down all essential oils, but some break down faster than others. For example, tea tree essential oil and others listed in Table 1 are more likely to oxidize than other essential oils. Citrus oils are also very vulnerable to destruction by oxygen because they are very high in limonene. On the other hand, essential oils that are very high in antioxidants such as eugenol, thymol, 1,8-cineole, and carvacrol are less likely to oxidize compared to other essential oils low in antioxidants. In order to avoid oxygen in the bottles, I will often combine multiple half-empty bottles of the same essential oil to protect the remaining oil from exposure to oxygen.

While the impact of light on essential oils is not as well documented as the impact of heat and air, one study demonstrates that as little as 50 minutes under UV light at 20°C can cause significant changes to sweet orange oil. The changes were not only degradation of existing compounds, but the synthesis of at least one dozen novel compounds.

To prevent your essential oils from changing chemical constituents quickly, store them properly away from heat, cold, light, and with the lid tightly shut.

ESSENTIAL OILS THAT CAN OXIDIZE AND INCREASE THE RISK OF SKIN IRRITATION	
Angelica	Frankincense
Anise	Galbanum
Caraway	Juniper
Celery	Lemon balm
Cistus	Myrtle
Citrus fruit oils	Pepper
Cypress	Pine
Dill oils	Sage
Elemi	Spruce
Fennel	Star anise
Fir oils	Tea Tree
Fleabane	Verbena

#7

DO ESSENTIAL OILS CONTAIN VITAMINS, PROTEINS, OR ENZYMES?

CARROT SEED
Daucus carota sativa

Short Answer

With very rare exception, essential oils do not usually contain any of these molecules.

Long Answer

With very rare exception, essential oils do not usually contain any of these vitamins, proteins, or enzymes. Let's recall that constituents that pass through distillation processes must be small (usually less than 500 amu) and heat stable (able to withstand temperatures above boiling (212°F/100°C) for a short period of time. Proteins and enzymes are large molecules that cannot rise and pass over the distillation process, and they are heat labile and break down very easily when exposed to heat. Expressed oils such as citrus oils could theoretically contain trace amounts of proteins; however, the presence or absence of proteins or enzymes does not affect the chemistry because these large molecules do not pass through the skin or enter the body when applied to the skin.

While smaller vitamins such as vitamin C are small enough to pass through distillation and theoretically could be found in essential oils, most small vitamins are water soluble compounds not likely to be compatible with fatty essential oils. There is a theoretical chance that the fat-soluble vitamins A, D, E, and K could be present in essential oils; however this is rare and should not occur on a regular basis, if ever. Because they are cold-pressed, citrus oils may contain larger molecules such as the vitamin beta-carotene, but the amount is so low that it could not be considered a dietary source of beta-carotene.

#8

DO ALLERGIES TO ESSENTIAL OILS EXIST?

THYME
Thymus vulgaris

Short Answer

Skin irritation, sensitization, and photosensitization are possible with many natural products including essential oils.

Long Answer

An allergy is an abnormal reaction to an ordinarily harmless substance called an allergen. When you have an allergy to something, your body views the allergen as an invader and attacks it. There are four different types of sensitization reactions that can all be classified as allergies. Very old oils or oils that have not been stored properly can oxidize, and this increases the risk for skin reactions of all types.

THE FOUR HYPERSENSITIVITY REACTIONS

Type I reactions occur when IgE antibodies attach themselves to mast cells, thereby releasing histamine. Histamine induces a wide variety of symptoms including an itchy and runny nose, sneezing, and watery eyes, as well as rash, eczema, hives, itchy skin, and asthma. In severe cases, type I reactions can lead to anaphylaxis where there is rash, severe asthma, alterations in heart rate, sense of impending doom, and swelling of the throat or mouth. Cinnamaldehyde and other essential oil constituents have been shown to cause type I allergic reactions, but they are rarely serious. Anaphylaxis is the most severe form of Type I allergic reaction, and there have only been two recorded anaphylactic reactions to fragrance molecules: one from isolated essential oil compounds blended into a perfume going through pre-sales testing, and another report of a nurse who was assaulted by a patient who sprayed three pumps of an unknown perfume in her face.

Type II reactions are when the immune system binds to antigens on the body's cell surface. The cells are recognized by macrophages and cause a B-cell response where antibodies are produced against the antigen. These reactions are similar to autoimmune diseases because in hypersensitivity reactions, it is a foreign drug metabolite being adsorbed onto the surface of the cell recognized as foreign versus attacking of self on the surface of cells. Type III reactions are when IgG or IgM react with an antigen and form immune complexes. There is no evidence of fragrance materials causing Type II or Type III allergic reactions.

Type IV reactions are delayed hypersensitivity reactions where there is no reaction to the first exposure to a substance, but subsequent exposures to the substance elicits a response. The first exposure is called the induction phase, and it usually takes about 10-15 days for a response to show. The subsequent exposure is the elicitation or challenge phase. The induction phase may take place close to the time of the elicitation phase, or it may take place years before elicitation. The most common cause of this type of hypersensitivity is poison ivy, but it may be caused by medications, household cleaners, cosmetics, and more.

Type IV reactions are the product of allergenic chemicals called haptens. Haptens – from the Greek word meaning 'to fasten' – are small molecules that combine with proteins and elicit the productions of antibodies. Haptens enter the body through the skin and bind with peptides on the Langerhans cells. The hapten-peptide complexes migrate to the local lymph node where T-cells learn to recognize hapten-peptide complexes as an antigen. Upon subsequent exposure, haptens are taken up by skin cells already bearing the hapten-peptide complexes, and T-cells activate in the dermis and epidermis. This initiates an immune response that releases cytokines and histamine and triggers cell death. Immune cells are recruited to the site, which then amplifies the reaction. This is sometimes why even the smallest exposure can lead to large reactions seemingly out of line with the level of exposure. There are many reports of fragrance materials causing Type IV hypersensitivity reactions, so let's review the data.

SUBCATEGORIES OF TYPE IV REACTIONS

Type IV reactions are further subdivided into allergic contact dermatitis and pigmented contact dermatitis. Allergic contact dermatitis is the most common type of delayed hypersensitivity. Allergic contact dermatitis from airborne volatile molecules is exceedingly rare, representing less than 0.2% of all cases. Skin reactions following application of an essential oil are much more common. Thankfully, if a reaction occurs, it is usually localized to the area of skin exposed to the haptens. People with skin reactions to fragrance are at greater risk for eye and airway symptoms if exposed to the fragrance in the air. Pigmented contact dermatitis is triggered by the same process, but instead of the skin getting red, it gets darker as melanin rises to the upper dermis. People with darker skin color are more likely to have this type of reaction, and women are more likely than men. This reaction is distinct from photosensitivity because it does not require UV light.

Photoallergy is a rare reaction where the skin reacts with UV light, but the skin's pigmentation does not change. There are several fragrance materials that are not found in essential oils that are banned from use in fragrance because of the risk of photoallergy. Many consider that photoallergy is impossible with essential oils, but there has been one case with sandalwood essential oil and one case with lavender essential oil reported. Given the extreme rarity of photoallergy, it is unlikely to be a concern for most essential oil users.

On the other hand, phototoxicity is common with essential oils, and new users of essential oils should be educated on the risk. Botanicals that can cause toxicity are in the Rutaceae family and Apiaceae family. Oils known to be phototoxic are bergamot, fig leaf, grapefruit, lemon (expressed, not distilled), lime (expressed, not distilled), orange, mandarin, rue, angelica, and cumin. Other citrus essential oils like lemon leaf, mandarin, sweet orange, satsuma, tangerine, tangelo, and yuzu are not considered to be phototoxic. Lower risk oils are clementine, combava, skimmia, angelica absolute, celery leaf, celery seed absolute, cumin seed absolute, khella, lovage, and parsnip. The risk of phototoxicity can be greatly reduced by removing the furanocoumarins (FCs).

FCs are known to intercalate (squeeze in between base pairs) in DNA. When exposed to UV light, the FCs form covalent bonds with DNA, which results in cross-linking of DNA (Figure 1). This causes an inflammatory response resulting in redness of the skin, sunburn, and blistering in severe cases. The reaction may be delayed for several days following exposure, and the hyperpigmentation may last for weeks.

In a study of 63 volunteers, differences in eye color, age, sex, or ability to tan did not affect phototoxic responses to bergamot oil. However, it took a higher concentration of bergamot oil to affect dark brown or black skin when compared to fair, sallow, or light brown. A suntan at baseline did confer some protection. People with albinism are at a very high risk for photosensitization, and they should exercise additional precautions.

Allergic contact dermatitis has been reported since the 1970s, and a fragrance mix has been used to test for allergies to essential oil. I am not thrilled with the way the data was generated. Instead of whole essential oil, the fragrance mix is a blend of essential oil chemical constituents blended together in 87% petrolatum. When using this mix, 11.4% of people are deemed to be allergic or sensitive to fragrance on average. However, when sandalwood, cedarwood, peppermint, spearmint or pine essential oils are used at a dilution of 2-10%, the average risk is less than 0.9%. There is much discussion online that ylang ylang and lemongrass can cause allergic reactions in some people, but it is important to note that this data was generated using people with a diagnosis of dermatitis at baseline, so it is not applicable to the general population.

Risk factors for skin sensitivity include health status, age, gender, and genetics. People who are chronically stressed are at greater risk because the immune system is ramped up. Children less than 3 months of age as well as women between the ages of 20-60 are at greater risk. Women are 3-4 times more likely than men to be affected by fragrances than men. Those lacking the ability to produce metabolizing enzymes are also at risk. Risk of reaction is also contingent on the substance applied, how it was applied, and whether the area was occluded.

All of this is a very long way of saying that whether you choose to call them allergies or sensitivities, some of the chemical constituents in essential oils, as well as whole oils, have been documented to cause inflammatory responses on the skin. The conclusions from the data do not necessarily account for if the oil was synthetic, fractionated, or adulterated, nor does it account for if it was compounded in a cosmetic or with a medication.

In my opinion, there are three take-home messages from this discussion:

1. Teach people about photosensitivity and the essential oils that can cause it. Nobody likes a sunburn.

2. If an essential oil is ever uncomfortable on the skin, apply carrier oil as often as needed.

3. If you have sensitive skin or would like to be extra cautious, dilute the essential oil in carrier oil before applying and consider a patch test (see question 2 for details on how to perform).

#9

WHERE CAN I LOOK FOR CREDIBLE INFORMATION ABOUT ESSENTIAL OILS?

BLUE CYPRESS
Callitris intratropica

Short Answer

There are dozens of resources and cited materials in this book, all of which are reputable sources of information about essential oils and natural medicine in my opinion.

Long Answer

There are dozens of resources and cited materials in this book, all of which are reputable sources of information about essential oils and natural medicine in my opinion. For day-to-day learning, I do what most everyone else does: I Google it (insert search engine of your choosing). When I want to go a step further, I look at Google Scholar or PubMed. I find that PubMed typically has papers that are more on topic for my searches, but Google Scholar offers more search results that link to papers available for free. PubMed has the additional benefit of having highly customizable filter options that can narrow search results from thousands to hundreds or even fewer.

Another reference I love is Natural Medicines Database. It is expensive, but excellent if you want a lot of information. It is easy to search for almost any herb, and the monographs are extensively researched and referenced. Be aware that the monographs are for herbs, not essential oils, so you must be careful to sift through the data correctly to ensure that you do not draw a conclusion tied to the herb and link it to the essential oil.

While I do not agree with all of his conclusions, *Essential Oil Safety* by Robert Tisserand is a powerful reference tool. I choose to use my own experiences with essential oils and ignore some of his advice, but have learned extensively from his work.

Further works by Kurt Schnaubelt, Gary Young, David Stewart, and Jane Buckle have also influenced my understanding on essential oil usage and interactions with the body.

Though not a book about essential oils, much of my knowledge of Eastern medicine herbs, foods, and healing has come from the text *Healing with Whole Foods* which is, for me, a life-changing text.

I continue to reference books from my pharmacy school days regularly: *Neuroscience*, *Drug Delivery Mechanisms*, *Netter's Anatomy*, and *Essential Reproduction* all reinforce my understanding of molecular diffusion, anatomy and physiology, and hormone function. None of these are light reads, but are essential for my background knowledge.

It is essential that one reviews commentary from blogs and social media websites with a cautionary eye. While Pinterest will give you lots of ideas, not all of the recommendations are backed up with evidence.

#10

WHAT ARE THE BEST WAYS TO TRAVEL WITH ESSENTIAL OILS?

ELEMI
Canarium luzonicum

— *Short Answer* —

Seal the bottles tightly, prevent them from getting too hot, consider a nifty carrying case, and be aware of which airport you are flying in and out of (some are super strict; others simply don't care).

Long Answer

I recommend never leaving home without a few essential oils. Traveling exposes us to new foods, new aromas, and new experiences – all of which can be good or bad. Peppermint essential oil under the arms on a hot bus in Indonesia, lavender essential oil on the skin after a day at the beach in Kota Kinabalu, or clary sage while clutching for dear life in a taxi swerving up the side of a mountain in the Dominican Republic can all be life savers while on the road. Take the essential oils that you use the most with you, and be sure to screw the lid on tight. Nothing is worse than opening luggage and realizing that an entire bottle has spilled on the journey.

It is important on car journeys to remember to bring your oils inside with you instead of leaving them in a hot car. Heat can change the chemical composition of essential oils, which can then change the aroma or the effect on the body. Some essential oils oxidize in response to heat, and this can increase the risk for skin irritation (e.g. angelica, celery, cypress, fir, myrtle, spruce, tea tree, and more). Another great tip for car journeys is to bring along a cotton pad or car diffuser. You can make a simple diffuser simply by dropping a few drops of essential oil on a cotton pad and placing it in the air vent of your car (works best in the summer when cold air is blown versus the winter when warm air is blown). Orange, tangerine, and other lively essential oils can reinvigorate the environment and help keep you alert on the road.

If you are traveling on a plane, you may bring essential oils in your carry-on luggage. Most suggestions from the Transportation Security Administration (TSA) state that you can bring no more than a quart-sized bag full of liquids, and that all the liquids must be less than three ounces. In my travels,

I have found that (in the United States) TSA doesn't care that much about the number of small liquids, but they do care if the liquids are larger than three ounces. TSA Precheck is also very helpful for frequent travelers because you won't have to take the liquids out of your bag.

In London, on the other hand, security will make you throw away any liquids that do not fit into a quart-sized bag or are over 3 ounces (and they are not nice about it at all). Other airports and security agents vary from almost no security in some African nations, to arguably the strictest airport security in the world in Srinagar or Tel Aviv. If I am in an airport I don't know well, I find it is easier just to ask a security agent because I don't how strict the airport is.

If you want to take more essential oils than will fit in a quart sized bag, you may consider getting some very small vials and a carrying case. There are so many carrying cases out there that can easily fit in a carry-on or in checked luggage. I find soft side cases a bit easier to manage in luggage, but hard side cases much more durable and lock easily.

There are some people who worry that sending essential oils through an x-ray scanner will change the frequency of the essential oils, but in my experience, I have never noticed a change in aroma or effectiveness after sending an essential oil through an x-ray scanner, even after repeated exposures to x-rays.

Some people give the advice to never use essential oils on a plane, and I find this to be rubbish advice. I have used essential oils on hundreds of flights, and I have never once had a complaint. In fact, it is much more likely to spark a conversation than garner ire from the person next to you. I love a drop of cinnamon or eucalyptus essential oil on a scarf, and I use cinnamon and clove essential oils in alcohol to spray down tray tables. I use the same mixture to spray my hands after using the airplane bathroom because some studies have shown that the water on the plane is so dirty you may walk away with more bacteria after washing your hands than before washing (It is non-potable for a reason. For real, don't brush your teeth with that water please. It is super gross.).

In conclusion, essential oils are the perfect traveling companion. Be sure that you take a couple everywhere you go and that you treat them well on the road.

Essential Oil Chemistry & Physiology

In this section, we will review some technical information about the chemistry and physiology of essential oils. There is a lot of highly technical language, so please use the glossary freely as you read. Question number four in section one is very helpful as background reading before you get started in this section.

#11

HOW DO WE PERCEIVE SMELLS?

ROSE
Rosa damascena

Short Answer

Odors interact with the hairs inside the nose, which prompts an electrical signal to be sent to the olfactory bulb and then deeper into the brain for interpretation.

Long Answer

Olfaction, or the sense of smell, is the oldest of all the sensory systems, but it remains one of the least understood. While other mammals such as dogs and cats are equipped with a much better sense of smell than humans, the human genome is nevertheless packed with over 950 odorant receptor genes (versus 1500 in the mouse) that comprise 3-5% of our genetic code.

Stimuli that activate olfaction are odorants, and they interact directly with the lining of the nose (olfactory epithelium). Odorant molecules like those found in essential oils are volatile, which means their small molecular weight enables them to rise quickly into the air, bringing their aroma with them.

Within the lining of the nose, there are receptor cells and support cells. The receptor cell has two distinct ends. On the side facing the outside world, there are tiny hairs known as cilia, and on the other end is an axon that connects directly to the olfactory bulb. When the cilia perceive an odorant molecule, an electrical current is generated and transmitted through the receptor cell. The cilia are so sensitive that a much larger current is generated when an odorant hits the cilia versus when it hits the receptor cell body. The odorant activates a receptor protein on the cilia that sends a signal to the second messenger, which opens a channel and allows calcium to flow through the channel. This generates an action potential that is sent upward to the olfactory bulb (Figure 1).

Not all receptor cells are the same. Certain receptors respond very strongly to aromas whereas others do not. For example, when three neurons are exposed to the aromas of cineole, isoamyl acetate, acetophenone, neuron 1 responds strongly to all three aromas but not with the same intensity or duration. Neuron 2 only produces a response to cineole, but it is intense and rapid. Neuron 3 does not respond to cineole, has a moderate response to isoamyl acetate, but has a large rapid response to acetophenone. Receptors that have similar intensity responses can be found together in clumps in the olfactory epithelium.

Above the receptor cells, axons project directly to the neurons that make up the olfactory nerve (also known as cranial nerve 1). The primary axon projections bring information to spherical glomeruli. Within each glomerulus, the axons of receptor cells contact the dendrites of mitral cells. Mitral cells send an elaborate tuft of dendritic projections that synapse with the primary olfactory axons. Mitral cells converge in a bundle, known as the lateral olfactory tract, that projects into the olfactory nuclei, olfactory tubercle, portions of the amygdala, and the entorhinal cortex. The olfactory tract also sends information to its major target: the pyriform cortex in the temporal lobe of the brain. Nerves in the pyriform cortex, olfactory tubercle, amygdala, and the entorhinal cortex respond to odors, and convey information to thalamic and hypothalamic nuclei and the orbitofrontal cortex, and the entorhinal cortex further relays information to the hippocampal formation. Though the signaling pathways are not fully understood, chemical and electrical signals initiated by odors reach a large variety of forebrain regions, allowing odors to influence cognitive, visceral, emotional, and homeostatic behaviors.

In conclusion, we perceive smells via an elaborate system of electrical impulses that travel from the receptor cells in the nose into the limbic system, and then to the forebrain for cognitive interpretation.

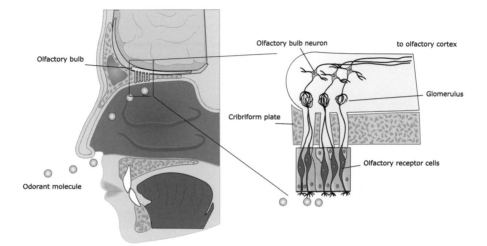

FIGURE 1: The Olfactory System

#12

CAN ESSENTIAL OIL MOLECULES ENTER THE BRAIN?

ROMAN CHAMOMILE
Chamaemelum nobile

― *Short Answer* ―

While chemicals in essential oils have many of the characteristics necessary to pass into the brain tissue, they must pass a formidable barrier: the blood-brain barrier.

Long Answer

As described in the previous question, there is an elaborate system by which odorants activate electrical signals in the brain. If a molecule from an essential oil is in the blood and attempts to pass into the brain tissue, it must pass a formidable blockade known as the blood-brain barrier. The blood-brain barrier prevents unwanted compounds from entering the brain, and allows desirable compounds such as water, some gases (e.g. oxygen), and other small, fatty molecules to pass via diffusion. There are also active pumps that ensure the uptake of molecules necessary for nourishment such as glucose and amino acids.

The blood-brain barrier is comprised of endothelial cells fused with tight junctions and surrounded by support cells known as astrocytes and pericytes. Combined, these structures prevent unwanted molecules from passing into the brain.

The endothelial cells of the blood-brain barrier are different than other endothelial cells because they lack fenestrae (windows that allow molecules to pass through), have reduced pinocytotic activity (carrier vessels that grab a compound from one side and move it to the other), have increased mitochondria (which provides energy needed for the active uptake of glucose and other necessary molecules), and contain high numbers of tight junctions.

The tight junctions are primarily responsible for the function of the blood-brain barrier. Tight junctions are formed between two closely associated endothelial cells with a network of parallel sealing strands of protein that prevent paracellular transport (movement of molecules between cells). The tight junctions are so strong that even the movements of ions like Na+ and Cl-

(sodium and chloride) can be prevented, and it thereby creates an additional electrical resistance. The tight junctions also polarize the endothelial cell, further intensifying the barrier.

Astrocytes are star-shaped cells that surround capillaries of the brain and act as support cells. While the tight junctions are primarily responsible for the function of the blood-brain barrier, the astrocytes are important in the regulation of fluid, electrolyte, amino acid, and neurotransmitter balance in the neuronal environment. Astrocytes are also important for creating and maintaining the endothelial cell barrier function.

Pericytes cover the endothelium substantially but incompletely, and modulate cerebral blood flow. They are also important in the formation of new blood vessels and formation of the vascular tree.

Molecules that can pass the blood-brain barrier are typically small and lipid soluble, as these are favorable characteristics for passing across a membrane (transmembrane diffusion). Molecular size is important when passing the blood-brain barrier. The largest molecule known to pass the blood-brain barrier is 7,800 amu, however many authors agree that it is tougher for compounds larger than 400-600 amu to cross. Common chemical constituents in essential oils such as monoterpenes have a molecular weight of 136 amu, sesquiterpenes 204 amu, and phenols 136 amu and above. The size of most molecules in essential oil usually do not exceed 500 amu, as it is difficult to distill molecules this large into essential oils.

Essential oils are lipid-soluble, and are more able to pass across cells than water soluble compounds; however, to enter the brain, a compound must pass through the cell membrane and then into the aqueous portion of the brain's interstitial fluid. Compounds that are too lipid-soluble can be held in the capillary, so there must be balance.

Essential oil molecules can effectively pass the blood-brain barrier due to their small size, compact shape, and balance between lipo- and hydrophilicity. Therefore essential oil molecules do enter the brain.

#13

HOW DO ESSENTIAL OILS INTERACT WITH BACTERIA?

CLOVE
Syzygium aromaticum

Short Answer

Essential oils interact with bacteria in many ways, and the interactions depend on the structure of the essential oil and on the structure of the bacteria.

Long Answer

Essential oils interact with bacteria in many ways, and the interactions depend on the structure of the essential oil and on the structure of the bacteria. We have learned some about the structure of essential oils in 5-carbon isoprene units, so let's move on and discuss the structure of bacteria.

Bacteria structures are commonly described as either gram-positive or gram-negative. Gram-positive bacteria have a thick peptidoglycan layer that stains purple in response to iodide, whereas gram-negative bacteria have a very thin peptidoglycan layer and do not stain purple. Because the peptidoglycan layer is very hydrophobic, it is easier for essential oil molecules to move from the outside of the cell to the inside of the cell.

Gram-negative bacteria are more complex structures than gram-positive bacteria. While they do contain a thin peptidoglycan layer, it is sandwiched between two cell membrane layers. The outer layer and the peptidoglycan are firmly connected with a lipoprotein. The outer membrane has openings known as porins that allow hydrophilic molecules to flow freely through the membrane.

Suffice it to say, gram-positive bacteria are much more hydrophobic (hate water/love fat), than their gram-negative, hydrophilic (love water/hate fat) counterparts. Because peptidoglycan is primarily hydrophobic, other hydrophobic molecules like those in essential oils can more easily penetrate through the cell wall into the cytoplasm of the bacteria, whereas in gram-negative bacteria, hydrophobic molecules move more slowly across porins and across the outer membrane. Therefore, gram-positive bacteria are more susceptible to destruction by essential oils than gram-negative bacteria.

In general, disruption of the cell membrane is the primary mechanism by which essential oils are described to act on bacteria. As the cell membrane is responsible for providing a barrier to the outside world, maintaining the energy status of the cell, transducing energy, moving solutes like salts, regulating metabolism, and maintaining turgor pressure, disruption of the cell membrane can be very detrimental to the bacteria and perhaps lead to cell death. In addition to disrupting the bacterial cell membrane, essential oils have been shown to degrade the cell wall, damage cytoplasmic membranes, induce cytoplasmic coagulation, damage membrane proteins, destroy the electron transport system, reduce intracellular ATP, and increase the leak of cellular contents. Essential oil molecules may hit one or more of these targets to carry out their action against bacteria.

No one essential oil compound acts the same across all varieties of bacteria, and it is difficult to predict susceptibility of one species, and can be difficult to predict susceptibility of different strains within the same species.

While essential oils can interact with and even kill bacteria, bacteria do not seem to have the same ability to create resistance to essential oils as they can to antibiotics.

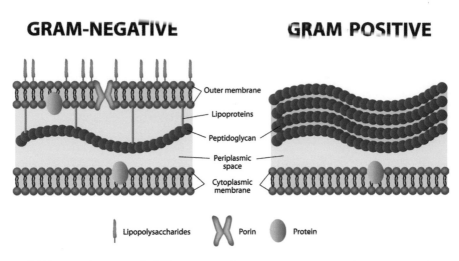

FIGURE 1: Structural differences of gram-negative and gram-positive bacteria

Essential Oil Usage

In this section, we will review questions about how to use essential oils on the skin and some more controversial usage models such as instillation in the eye.

#14

IS THERE A BEST WAY TO USE AN OIL?

JADE LEMON
Citrus limon eureka var. formosensis

Short Answer

There is no perfect way to use an essential oil, and your choice may vary depending on what you wish to accomplish with the application.

Long Answer

Essential oils may be used in a variety of ways including aromatically, topically, and by ingestion. Aromatically is the simplest way to use an essential oil, whether by direct inhalation via diffusion or nebulization. Direct inhalation is simply inhaling the essential oil directly from the bottle. Diffusion disperses essential oils throughout the air. Typically, diffusers use electricity to propel molecules a greater distance, though diffusion may also be accomplished by adding a few drops of oil to a cotton ball or piece of paper. Depending on the diffuser device, diffusion can carry a light aroma of essential oils up to 100 feet away from the source. Atomizing diffusers or nebulizers directly disperse essential oils into the air without the use of paper or water as a dispersant. Because essential oils are being dispersed without a dispersant, an intense aroma is created in the area closest to the nebulizer.

Essential oils may also be used topically (applied directly to the skin). Carrier oils are an excellent addition when using essential oils this way. Carrier oils are fatty oils such as almond, olive, jojoba, coconut, etc. that ensure that the application of essential oils is comfortable to the skin. Many essential oils are mild and gentle and do not necessitate the use of a carrier oil, but others may be perceived as either hot or cold to the skin. Some examples are oregano, lemongrass, peppermint, cinnamon, clove, and cassia. If an oil ever feels too cool or too warm on the skin, adding carrier oil will help pull the essential oil away from the skin. It is also important to avoid adding water to the skin if an oil feels too warm or too cool, as this will further drive the oil into the skin and may worsen the discomfort. Carrier oils are especially important when using essential oils on infants, children, and anyone who is not an experienced oil user. If ever in doubt, never be shy to use carrier oil as often as needed to ensure that using the oil doesn't cause discomfort.

Essential oils may also be directly ingested or used as a flavoring for foods and beverages, and many are generally recognized as safe for consumption by the Food and Drug Administration. When directly ingesting oils, it is important to note that the flavor may be very pungent and may or may not reflect the aroma of the oil. As a food flavoring, a little essential oil can go a very long way. One to two drops may be all that is needed to flavor an entire dish. You may also dip the end of a toothpick in an essential oil and stir into the food immediately before serving to ensure that the flavor does not overwhelm the food.

There is not perfect way to use essential oils; it simply depends on the outcome that you wish to achieve. If you want to refresh, enliven, or transform a space, diffusion may be the best option. If you want an intense aromatic experience to accompany meditation or intuitive thought, directly inhaling the oil may be the most effective means to this end. If you want to promote healthy skin or use an essential oil as a perfume, then apply directly to the skin. Lastly as a digestif or a food flavoring, ingestion may be the best possible usage mechanism.

#15

WHERE SHOULD I APPLY ESSENTIAL OILS ON MY SKIN?

WINTERGREEN
Gaultheria procumbens

Short Answer

Most skin is relatively the same; however, use caution when applying essential oils to private parts, the face, under the arms, and on children (especially premature infants) and the elderly.

Long Answer

There is no specific place where essential oils should or should not be applied. Before applying essential oil to the skin, you may consider permeability and skin sensitivity. It is also prudent to consider what you would like the essential oil to do for you. For example, if you would like to support the delicate skin around your eyes, it is likely a good choice to apply the essential oil in that area versus applying to the feet, where it will have a more challenging time beautifying the skin on your face. Permeability is how easily a substance (such as an essential oil) moves across a barrier (such as the skin). In normal, unbroken adult skin, most areas of the skin are equal in terms of permeability. However, there is variation across different parts of the body. The nail is the least permeable piece of skin, followed by the palms of the hands and the soles of the feet, followed by limbs and trunk, followed by the face and scalp (I include the backs of the ears in this group), followed by the scrotum, which is the most permeable bit of skin.

Permeability of skin does change throughout the lifetime, and it is important to use caution when applying essential oils to the skin of infants (especially premature infants). In an in vitro study of skin cells from infants 25-41 weeks' gestation and up to eight days old, sodium salicylate was 100-1000 times more likely to cross the skin in preterm infants 30 weeks' gestation or less, and this could theoretically put a child at risk for accidental poisoning by substances applied to the skin. In a study of infants 25-41 weeks' gestation, aged 1 hour to 26 days, infants 37 weeks' gestation or later showed little to no absorption of a 1% or 10% solution of phenylephrine when applied to the skin, and had little water loss from the area. On the contrary, infants 32 weeks' gestation or less showed marked drug absorption and high skin water losses. Absorption fell steadily as infants aged, and by about 2 weeks of age, the skin of the most immature infants functioned like the skin of mature infants. The changes in permeability can be explained by the poor development of the stratum corneum (the tough outermost layer of skin) in premature infants and the rapid maturation of the stratum corneum after birth.

The data about changes in skin permeability in the elderly are mixed with some data suggesting differences in people older than 50 years old from people less than 30 years old, others suggesting differences in people older than 71 years old, and others suggesting no differences at all. There is some research that suggests the changes in absorption as we age is dependent upon the lipophilicity of the compound. For example, testosterone (a very lipophilic compound) is absorbed the same across skin of volunteers aged 22-40 years old and aged >65 years old. On the other hand, absorption of water-soluble compounds like caffeine and acetylsalicylic acid do significantly differ between subjects 22-40 years old and >65 years old, with younger subjects absorbing significantly more than their older counterparts. This data is in direct contradiction to in vitro studies of human cadaver skin, which conclude that skin from older adults (>66 years old) is 7 times more permeable to fluorescein than skin from younger adults (<29 years old), as well as to the observation that older skin absorbs more because as we age, the skin gets thin and frail. There is also evidence to suggest that absorption of chemicals across the skin is slower, but ultimately will match that of younger skin given enough time. Suffice it to say, we do not know the full story of how skin permeability changes with age. We also cannot conclude that skin from people of the same age is uniform, and there may be people with damaged skin who absorb more than their peers.

Long Answer

There is no essential oil that is perfect in any given situation for any individual person or any given reason, and even if an oil has worked effectively in the past, it may not be effective in the future. However, greater potential harm is possible with synthetic essential oils or oils with fillers or additives. Use of 100% pure essential oil is always recommended.

Before you purchase an essential oil, it is important to consider the quality. Markers of high quality essential oils include evidence of good farming practices and sustainability, and a higher price that reflects the workload as well as the volume of plants that it takes to produce essential oils.

Just as there is no perfect way to use essential oils, there is no best possible way to choose which essential oil is the best possible oil in each situation. You may find that you use a certain oil for the same reason repeatedly, but your tastes may change over time. If you are unsure of where to start, consider what you are trying to achieve with the application.

Here are a few suggestions if you do not know where to start. If you are tired; inhaling, diffusing, or ingesting peppermint oil is a great option (whereas something calming like clary sage could intensify the tiredness). If you want to keep your skin looking young, add a few drops of frankincense to your moisturizer each morning (whereas peppermint could be a bit intense and very cold, or clove or cinnamon would be too hot for this purpose). If you are using essential oil with your diffuser, pick an aroma that you like (not everyone wants a house that smells like ledum). If you are ingesting, select an essential oil that is labeled for that use, and start with a small amount of a tasty oil, like orange essential oil in your water, or fennel essential oil in a capsule. If you are applying to the skin, use caution with the hot oils, and always use carrier oil as needed. Lavender, rose, patchouli, Roman chamomile, sandalwood, and more are generally very gentle on the skin.

Long Answer

Essential oils can be applied directly to the skin. Many aromatherapy texts encourage dilution prior to any use on the skin; however, in my personal experience, direct application without dilution is appropriate in individuals who are experienced with essential oil usage. Dilution is prudent for children and anyone inexperienced with essential oils, and is strongly recommended in infants, especially premature infants who require heavy dilution, if essential oils are used at all. Dilution is also recommended when using oils that may be perceived as hot on the skin such as cinnamon, clove, oregano, and lemongrass.

If you have never used an essential oil and wish to take additional caution, you may perform a patch test prior to using an essential oil. To perform a patch test, apply 1-2 drops of essential oil to a patch of skin such as the forearm. Observe that area of skin over the course of 1-2 hours for any noticeable reaction; usually reactions occur within 5-10 minutes. If you experience a hot or burning sensation or if you develop a rash, add carrier oil to the affected area as often as needed.

If discomfort or irritation occurs, stop using the essential oil, and apply carrier oil, full fat milk, or breastmilk to the affected area. Never use water to flush the oil off the skin, as this may increase discomfort. If a rash occurs, this may be a sign of reaction with petrochemicals; drink adequate water to encourage the release and removal of body toxins. Toxins present in petrochemical-based soaps and skin care products, detergents and perfumes may trigger some reactions. Consider discontinuation of these agents if a reaction occurs. Before using the essential oil again, perform a patch test and dilute with carrier oil as needed.

If essential oil gets in your eye, flush with carrier oil to alleviate any discomfort. Discomfort should be alleviated within minutes. If eye discomfort does not subside within 5 minutes, please seek medical attention. Be aware that some government documents require that water be the only substance that should be used to dilute or flush away substances from the skin or the eye. I suggest against this advice, and advise to dilute with carrier oil as quickly as possible.

It is generally good practice to dilute essential oils before applying to pets, especially pets like cats who lack a P450 system. Space out the dosing for these animals as well, so instead of applying each day, you may apply every 2-3 days. Dogs absorb essential oils through their fur, so even diffusing may result in topical administration.

Long Answer

In my opinion, there is no one table of dilution ratios that is correct for every person. Each person has different skin, each mom has a different opinion about what is safe for her child, and each pet owner has a different opinion about what is safe for their pet. While I agree that it is prudent (likely necessary in premature infants) to dilute essential oils in carrier oil before using on sensitive skin or on someone who has never experienced essential oils, I do not think there is one perfect way to do it. There are a million different answers online, with some arguing that no essential oil should ever be applied neat and others contending that almost any essential oil can be applied neat. Schools of aromatherapy cannot create one consistent suggestion. And how could they? Everybody's skin is different.

What is more important than a table of dilution ratios is knowledge of which oils can be hot or cold on the skin and which oils may be more irritating to sensitive skin. Oils that may be hot on the skin include mustard, horseradish, massoia, cinnamon, clove, lemongrass, cassia, thyme, oregano, sage, pine, Siberian fir, marjoram, and blends that contain any of these oils. Peppermint has a dramatic cooling effect on the skin. If you choose to apply these oils to the skin, you may consider dilution. For the average adult, 1 drop of an essential oil in 10 drops of carrier oil is likely more than adequate dilution. However, if you find that you do not like the sensation of the oil on your skin, always have confidence to add more carrier oil.

If you are someone who wants a specific table of dilution ratios, here is one for you to utilize. However, this is by no means the only appropriate way to dilute. Use your judgment as you dilute.

DILUTION RATIOS FOR ESSENTIAL OILS FOR CHILDREN		
	Recommended %	Preparation
Premature infant	0.03% or less, may avoid completely. Choose very gentle oils.	1 drop in at least 100 ml carrier oil
Up to 3 months	0.1-0.2%	3-6 drops in 100 ml of carrier oil
3-24 months	0.25-0.5%	7-15 drops in 100 ml carrier oil
2-6 years old	1-2%	3-6 drops in 10 ml carrier oil
6-12 years old	2-5%	6-15 drops in 10 ml carrier oil
>12 years old	5% or more	15 or more drops in 10 drops carrier, or up to direct application without carrier oil

#19

CAN ESSENTIAL OILS BE INSTILLED IN THE EYE?

MYRRH
Commiphora myrrha

Short Answer

They can, but it requires extraordinary caution.

Long Answer

The instillation of essential oils into and around the eye is recommended in aromatherapy textbooks, however great care must be taken with this. Without great care, the eye can be damaged or you may experience significant side effects. Several fatty oil-based eye drops are available as over the counter medications as eye lubricants, and fatty oils are also used as carriers in some prescription eye drops. While some online blogs claim that there are a variety of vision problems that can be treated with essential oils, I have not seen this proven true by the data. In fact, data related to essential oils in and around the eye is limited, and it should be emphasized that the essential oil is always significantly diluted in each study.

If you choose to use essential oils in your eye, there are several very critical safety points that must be reiterated. First, essential oils must always be significantly diluted. While that dilution ratio is not precisely defined, for this purpose, one drop of a gentle essential oil in 50, 100 or more drops of carrier oil is reasonable. For any essential oil that is hot on the skin, you may choose to avoid use entirely. If you choose to accept the risk, dilution in 100, 200 or more drops of carrier oil is recommended. Failure to dilute the oil could result in serious side effects. It is advisable to purchase a specialty sterile carrier oil with a light to medium weight for dilution. Next, if you choose to instill the diluted drop, you are still accepting the risk for side effects including stinging, burning, redness, irritation, vision changes, and inflammation. Last, if any side effects become intolerable, never apply water to the eye. Always flush with additional carrier oil. Attempting to flush with water may worsen symptoms.

My opinion is to skip instillation of essential oils directly into the eye, and apply them around the eye instead.

#20

HOW DO I CHOOSE THE BEST DIFFUSER?

PETITGRAIN
Citrus aurantium amara

Short Answer

When choosing a diffuser, you can consider the diffusion mechanism, size of the space where the essential oil will be diffused, amount of oils required, convenience, and aesthetic.

Long Answer

When choosing a diffuser, you can consider the diffusion mechanism, size of the space where the essential oil will be diffused, amount of oils required, convenience, and aesthetic. There are three basic types of cold diffuser mechanisms: ultra-sonicating, nebulizing/atomizing, and evaporative. We will not cover heated essential oil diffusers as I do not encourage heating the essential oils during diffusion.

Ultra-sonicating diffusers use an electric current that causes a metal disk to vibrate at greater than 20 kHz, and this causes an agitation of liquid into the air. This type of diffuser commonly uses water as a base, and the water is diffused into the air along with the essential oil. Some diffusers call for distilled water, and some call for tap water. Distilled water contains fewer minerals and is less likely to clog the ultra-sonicating action in diffusers, but there are a few diffusers that run more efficiently with tap water. Personally, I have used tap water in many diffusers, and simply ensure that the sonicating disc is kept clean. When using an ultra-sonicating diffuser, it is important to keep the metal plate at the bottom of the diffuser clean, or you run the risk of damage to the diffuser.

Nebulizing diffusers do not use water as a base, but instead use high velocity compressed air to turn a liquid into an aerosol. Nebulizing diffusers typically use more essential oil per diffusion cycle than ultra-sonicating diffusers, but nebulizing diffusers produce a stronger aroma in the area surrounding diffuser. Some nebulizing diffusers may make more noise than ultra-sonicating diffusers, and may not be appropriate when diffusing in quiet environments. When using a nebulizing diffuser, it is important to carefully set the run timer and to ensure that you do not accidentally diffuse an entire bottle of oil too quickly.

Evaporative diffusers use a fan to waft essential oils into the air. Evaporative diffusers tend not to create as strong an aroma as other types of diffusers. However, they can be convenient when traveling (you can create your own evaporative diffuser by placing a few drops of essential oil on a cotton ball and placing it in the air vent of a car).

Convenience is especially important when traveling. There are USB diffusers that can easily slip into a carry-on bag, handbag or pocket. They use air to propel small particles of essential oil into the environment (nebulizing action), and they are perfect for busy travelers and car journeys. If you choose to take a larger diffuser on the road, select a diffuser made of plastic, as glass is too fragile and can easily be damaged during travel.

Diffusers come in many different aesthetic presentations. Diffusers may be made of metal, wood, or plastic; and each has a unique look and feel. Some diffusers can glow very brightly and double as a nightlight for small children. Diffusers may have unique covers that are designed to inspire the minds of children. Select a diffuser that is perfect for your environment.

#21

ARE THERE ANY PRECAUTIONS I SHOULD TAKE BEFORE DIFFUSING?

RUE
Ruta graveolens

Short Answer

Choose a smell that you like, and use caution if you are diffusing in a confined space with very young children or pets (especially cats) in the room.

Long Answer

When diffusing, it is important to select an aroma that you like and want your environment to smell like. Nothing is worse than filling a diffuser with an aroma that you don't love and then either having to deal with it for a while or pour it out. You may also consider what you are aiming to achieve with the use of the oil: if it is early in the morning and you need to get work done, diffusing oils that you find sedating may not be the best choice; if it is late in the evening and you want to go to sleep, diffusing essential oils that you find activating may not be the best choice.

Before diffusing an essential oil, you may wish to consider if there are pets in your home. Animals may be more sensitive to essential oils, and, since some animals absorb essential oils through their hair follicles, diffusion may inadvertently lead to a topical application. On the other hand, diffusion is one of the gentlest ways to introduce pets to essential oil because it is a small amount in their environment versus a drop directly on their skin. Some authors recommend that anise, garlic, horseradish, juniper, thyme, yarrow, and clove should never be used on pets, and suggest that lavender, cedarwood, chamomile, eucalyptus, myrrh, rose, ravintsara, and valerian and many others are safer options. Use caution with very young animals just as you would with a young child.

Additional caution should be exercised with cats. Cats lack the ability to glucuronidate substances (they cannot add a piece of a molecule that helps foreign substances to be eliminated) in the liver, and it is prudent to be cautious when diffusing oils that are high in phenols such as cassia, clove, oregano, thyme, and savory or essential oils high in monoterpenes such as citrus oils (excluding yuzu), pine, spruce and fir. It may also be prudent to give cats additional time between exposures as their metabolism and excretion is slower than other animals.

As with humans, quality is also key when selecting an essential oil to use on a pet. So, always select the highest quality essential oils with no additives or synthetics. If you choose to diffuse essential oils around a pet, observe the pet for any signs of discomfort such as increased breathing rate, panting, drooling, excessive scratching, squinting eyes, or anything out of the ordinary. If any of these symptoms occur, simply turn off the diffuser and give your animal access to fresh air. It is also prudent to keep the door to the room open so the animal can have the freedom to move into another room if they choose.

Some parents choose to avoid certain essential oils in their children. Gentle oils such as citrus oils, frankincense, tea tree and patchouli essential oil are recognized by most authors as safe to use with children. Eucalyptus and peppermint essential oils get a very bad reputation online for being dangerous for children; however, my analysis of the data leads me to believe that they are (as with most essential oils) only potentially harmful when used excessively or directly on the face (see the special populations section for more details). If you are a parent who chooses to avoid certain essential oils on your child's skin, you may also choose to avoid diffusing those oils.

There is a lengthy discussion in the disease interaction section about whether essential oils have the potential to cause lipid pneumonia, and that discussion extends to diffusing essential oils. The data ultimately leads me to the conclusion that they do not cause lipid pneumonia, and I have seen no data that leads me to believe that there is even a small risk.

#22

DOES COOKING OR ADDING AN ESSENTIAL OIL IN A BEVERAGE ALTER THE CHEMICAL PROFILE?

DILL
Anethum graveolens

Short Answer

Yes, but it does not mean that the essential oil is made harmful in the process. It simply means that it has relayed its aroma and taste to the food. Evidence suggests that the chemical profile may be changed less in the essential oil than in the whole plant containing the essential oil.

Long Answer

Yes, but it does not mean that the essential oil is made harmful in the process. It simply means that it has relayed its aroma and taste to the food. Evidence suggests that the chemical profile may be changed less in the essential oil than in the whole plant containing the essential oil.

Cooking with heat changes the chemical structure of all foods. For example, when you heat an egg, the proteins in the whites unfurl and bump into each other forming new bonds and stiffening into cooked egg white. The Maillard reaction between amino acids and reducing sugars gives grilled meats and the crusts of breads their distinctive brown color. Caramelization occurs as sugars are reduced and can transform a basic bowl of white sugar into a thick, creamy, brown caramel sauce.

We have already discussed how essential oils should be stored at ambient temperatures, as both cold and hot temperatures can change the chemical composition, shortening the oils' shelf life. Storage temperature is known to affect essential oil chemical composition with chemical reactions increasing with increasing temperature (approximately twice the chemical reactions per every 10°C rise in temperature). Auto-oxidation at high temperatures increases the risk for free radical formation, whereas low temperatures increase the solubility of oxygen (which may also lead to reduced shelf life and spoilage of oils). Interestingly, one study showed that terpenes do not necessarily change in the same way at temperatures above 100°C as they do at lower temperatures that are warmer than ambient temperature.

In a study of fresh oregano and thyme, and oregano and thyme essential oils, levels of thymol and carvacrol were measured after boiling and baking. Boiling the plant and the essential oil retained 20% more thymol and carvacrol than baking. Thyme essential oils retained 25% more thymol when the essential oil was used versus the fresh, ground thyme leaves. Conversely, oregano leaves retained 39% more carvacrol than the essential oil. This suggests that both essential oils in fresh plants and extracted essential oils will change through the cooking process, and that extracted essential oils may have different chemical reactions than essential oils inside the plant.

I have no data that leads me to believe that the changes to the essential oil constituents increases the risk for harm. It is simply that there will be a greater aroma in the room as the essential oils are cooked, and that the essential oils will impart flavor to food. If you are concerned about the chemical reactions, you may choose to add it near the end of the cooking process or choose to add into a room temperature beverage.

While most people inhale the aroma of an essential oil or rub it on their skin and have a pleasant experience, there can be some reactions to essential oils. In this section, we will cover reactions and what chemical constituents are most likely to cause them.

#23

WHAT ARE THE ESSENTIAL OILS THAT ARE MOST LIKELY TO CAUSE SKIN IRRITATION?

ONYCHA
Styrax benzoin

Short Answer

Many of the essential oil constituents that are the most irritating to the skin come from essential oils that are not widely available commercially, but others with more moderate irritation are. If ever an essential oil is irritating to the skin, please add carrier oil.

Long Answer

Certain constituents in essential oils can potentially cause skin irritation. High risk is conferred by allyl isothiocyanate, benzyl isothiocyanate, and the massoia lactone; and moderately irritating essential oils are benzoic acid, carvacrol, p-cresol, and thymol. For whole essential oils, the highest risk of irritation comes from horseradish, mustard, and massoia essential oil, followed by immortelle absolute, sage, and garlic essential oil. Lower, but still existent, risk for irritation comes from oregano, marjoram, savory, ajowan, fir, and pine essential oils.

Essential oils that are high in furanocoumarins and lactones can increase the risk for phototoxicity (sunburn), so use caution with bergamot, fig leaf, grapefruit, lemon, lime, orange, rue, cumin, angelica, and mandarin if you plan to be in the sun.

Many essential oils have been shown to potentially cause skin sensitization, so be cautious when applying elecampane, fig leaf, costus, massoia, saffron, lavandin absolute, cassia, cinnamon bark, and lavender absolute.

Even the gentlest of essential oils may be uncomfortable to the skin if the skin is irritated at baseline. Use caution on burns, broken skin, or inflamed skin, and consider using carrier oil in addition to the essential oil.

If an essential oil is ever uncomfortable on the skin, simply add carrier oil to the affected area as often as needed. You can never go wrong by adding more carrier oil.

#24

WHY DO SOME PEOPLE GET HEADACHES AFTER INHALING ESSENTIAL OILS?

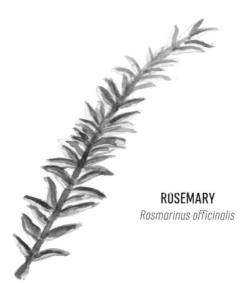

ROSEMARY
Rosmarinus officinalis

Short Answer

For migraine sufferers, aromas of all kinds can be triggers for migraine attacks. For people without migraines, there is no clear etiology for aromas causing other types of headaches.

Long Answer

Migraine headache is one of the only diseases associated with a change in olfactory perception at the onset of symptoms, and many migraine sufferers report an aversion to aromas during an attack, stating that perfumes and odors may be a trigger for migraine. Even between attacks, migraine sufferers may be more sensitive to aromas. Hormonal fluctuations (which are at least partially related to olfaction) are also a cause of migraine headaches, and women in their child-bearing years are more prone to headaches that younger women and men of all ages. Therefore, it is well known that in the setting of migraine, aromas, perfumes, and even essential oils can trigger a headache.

We also know that exposure to a high concentration of essential oil over a long period of time (more than 30 minutes) may cause a headache, but unless someone is nebulizing pure essential oil in a tented environment, this is not a common occurrence. In this instance, the headache is the result of exposure to a high concentration over an extended period and may be the body's way of giving a very early warning sign of overexposure. If this occurs, simply increase your exposure to fresh air.

The question then is why do some people who do not experience migraines get a headache after inhaling essential oils? A PubMed search of "essential oil and headache" revealed 29 articles. Many were unrelated to the topic, others were articles on the possible benefits of essential oils relieving headache, and none were reports of essential oils specifically causing headache. One article suggested that the *Pogostemon elsholtzioides* essential oil may cause vasorelaxation in phenylephrine-induced contractions in aortic rings. Given that anti-migraine medications such as the so-called triptan drugs act by mimicking serotonin and causing vasoconstriction of dilated vessels, if an essential oil has vasodilatory or vasorelaxant effects, this could be a potential mechanism of action for how an essential oil may cause headache. However, the data simply does not reflect this as a cause of headache. There are studies that show an increase in serotonin associated with essential oil inhalation, which again would not lend itself to a mechanism that would lead to headache.

Similar Google and Google Scholar results reveal studies that do not lead me to the conclusion that essential oils have a mechanistic reason for causing headache except in the arena of overuse. At the risk of sounding like a pseudoscientist, I question if the aversion to essential oils and subsequent headaches are a byproduct of emotions rather than the essential oil, given the lack of mechanistic rationale for essential oils causing headaches.

#25

HOW QUICKLY DO ESSENTIAL OILS ENTER THE BLOOD STREAM?

PALMAROSA
Cymbopogon martinii

───── *Short Answer* ─────

Quickly; however, it depends on many
factors such as dose and route.

Long Answer

The speed of essential oil absorption depends on many factors including route of administration, dose of administration, and duration of exposure.

Absorption through the skin is determined by several things: the surface area where the essential oil was applied, the duration of exposure, if the area was occluded (covered) after the essential oil was applied, the temperature of the skin, and the action of the metabolizing enzymes on the skin. As each of these increase, so too does the absorption of the essential oil. Furthermore, the skin of the face, neck, scalp, and wrist is a bit thinner than other skin, and this too may enhance absorption. Absorption following oral administration is dependent on dose and metabolizing enzyme activity in the gastrointestinal tract.

Following an oral dose of a medication containing the equivalent of 1.08 mg thymol in 20 healthy male volunteers of an average at of 29.5 ± 6.74 years, blood samples were obtained every 15 minutes for 1 hours, then every 30 minutes for an additional 3 hours, and then every hour for 8 additional hours, and then at hour 14, 24, 31, 38, 48, 55, 62, and 72; cumulative urine samples were obtained at hours 0-3, 3-6, 6-9, 9-14, 14-24, 24-31, 38-48, 48-55, 55-62, and 62-72 hours after administration. For the first 20 minutes after administration, only thymol could be detected in the serum, and after 20 minutes, thymol sulfate could also be detected. Free thymol was not found in the serum at any point, as it is rapidly cleaved to thymol sulfate; this is consistent with previous studies. The maximum serum concentration was found to be 1.97 hours for thymol sulfate. Both thymol sulfate and thymol glucuronide were found in the urine within 3 hours. Importantly, the medication included an extract of thyme instead of thyme

essential oil, but the thymol level was standardized in
each dose.

A study was conducted where two samples of lavender oil
in peanut oil (diluted to 25% and 30%) were applied to the
stomach of a healthy man, and then blood levels were drawn
immediately prior to the application, and then again at 5,
15, 30, 45, 60, 75 and 90 minutes. Gas chromatography and
mass spectrometry of the blood samples revealed that the
constituents of lavender oil, linalool, and linalyl acetate reached
maximum concentration in the blood at just under 20 minutes.
The same two constituents were metabolized to non-detectable
levels in approximately 90 minutes. The essential oil and fatty
oil blend gave numerically higher peak plasma concentrations
following application of the lower concentration of essential oil,
but it was not statistically or significantly different.

In a study of isolated alpha-humulene isolated from C.
verbenacea (black sage) administered orally, topically, and
intravenously in mice, plasma levels as well as tissue levels
from liver, kidney, heart, lungs, spleen and brain were
measured following administration. Oral bioavailability was
found to be 18%. The half-life was very short at 16.8 minutes
following oral administration, and 1.8 minutes after intravenous
administration; the elimination half-life was longer. Notable
levels of the compound were found in the liver, kidney, heart,
lungs, spleen, and brain half an hour after oral administration,
but these had decreased significantly by 4 hours. Therefore, this
study demonstrates that oral administration of alpha-humulene
is absorbed into multiple body tissues and eliminated over the
course of hours.

In conclusion, essential oils enter the blood and tissues in many
ways. They do so quickly, and they are eliminated quickly in
healthy people.

#26

HOW DO ESSENTIAL OILS IMPACT HORMONES?

CLARY SAGE
Salvia sclarea

Short Answer

Essential oils and essential oil constituents trigger electrical impulses that feed into the hypothalamus, and the hypothalamus is very important for balancing hormones. The answer to this question could go on endlessly; what follows will barely skim the surface of all the data available.

Long Answer

The answer to this question could go on endlessly. There are so many different studies of essential oils and their constituents. To narrow the data, I excluded discussions of non-mammal animal species. I limited the discussion to thyroid, male and female reproductive hormones, and hormones associated with stress response, thereby excluding data related to blood, insulin balance, and bone homeostasis. I also excluded most in vitro data, except to round out the discussion on receptor binding. While in other parts of this I venture into discussion about plant extracts and fatty acids/fatty oils when data on essential oil is lacking, this section excludes any data except what is related to essential oils. I also eliminated data related to estrous cycles in non-primates, and data published before 1980.

WOMEN'S HEALTH

In rats with drug-induced polycystic ovarian syndrome, white cedar essential oil (high in α- and β-thujone, fenchone, and sabinene, and chemically similar to red cedar) significantly decreased testosterone and luteinizing hormone while increasing estradiol and progesterone. It also decreased low density cholesterol along with glucose and leptin.

In a small number of women with a mild increase in body hair on the face, neck, chest and other areas typically associated with male body hair, lavender oil and tea tree oil sprayed twice a day for three months decreased both the amount and diameter of hair, and did not produce any effects on hormones.

When niaouli essential oil is applied to the to the skin, it promotes increased absorption of estradiol across the skin. This may lead to greater pharmacologic action of estradiol.

Menstrual cycles of women can be synchronized when living with other women, and this effect is likely driven by the various aromas given off during different phases of the menstrual cycle.

Certain essential oil constituents have been shown to have estrogenic activity in vitro such as citral, geraniol, and nerol, and some with anti-estrogenic, eugenol, but none of these compounds showed any ability to induce uterine hyperplasia or change uterine vascular flow. Therefore, the clinical significance of the interaction is unknown.

There is an in-depth review of hormone receptor binding capacity in the section on pregnancy.

MEN'S HEALTH

As discussed in the section on essential oils in pregnancy, it is highly unlikely that any essential oil can inhibit male fertility; however, there are chemical substances and medications that can wreak havoc on male reproduction. Animal studies of impact of essential oils on male fertility are usually in animals where substances known to be harmful to male fertility are used to cause harm, and the essential oil's protective effect is measured against a control.

For example, the chemotherapeutic taxane drugs (paclitaxel and docetaxel) are well known to cause changes in sperm count and quality, decreased weight of testes, and change testicular and epididymal balance (the epididymis is a duct behind the testis by which sperm passes on the way to the vas deferens and urethra on its way out of the body). The co-administration of cinnamon bark essential oil with the taxanes has been shown to protect against these damages in rat models.

In another study aimed at examining celery essential oil's ability to protect against testicular damage associated with DEHP (di-(2-ethylhexyl) phthalate), celery essential oil alleviated testicular atrophy, aspermia of the seminiferous tubules, and vacuole degeneration.

Rosemary essential oil and *Lavandula stoechas* were both shown to protect against oxidative stress and markers of reproductive organ damage (as evidenced by decreased weight of testes, and sperm quality decline) in alloxan-induced diabetes.

In healthy rats exposed to inhalation of formaldehyde alone or formaldehyde plus lavender oil, formaldehyde had a significantly negative impact on the male reproductive system as evidenced by decreased epididymal sperm concentrations, decreased sperm motility, and abnormal sperm rates. In the group that inhaled lavender oil alongside the formaldehyde, abnormal sperm rates were significantly decreased and sperm mobility and sperm concentrations were significantly increased.

THYROID HEALTH

The impact of 60 mg/kg of chasteberry essential oil in sterile olive oil injected subcutaneously into rats for three weeks on thyroid function was compared to injection of olive oil alone. In the animals that received the chasteberry extract, the data showed that they had higher density of thyrotrophs (cells that produce thyroid stimulating hormone) in the pituitary gland, higher levels of thyroid stimulating hormone in the serum, increased volume of follicular epithelium (the cells responsible for the secretion of thyroid hormone), higher levels of circulating thyroid hormone, higher levels of the sodium-iodide symporter (the transporter than is the first step in the creation of thyroid hormone), and all of these measures were statistically significant. On the other hand, corticotrophs (the cells that secrete adrenocorticotropic hormone, ACTH, which then goes on to stimulate the adrenal glands) decreased, and circulating levels of ACTH were low. This data indicates that chasteberry essential oil can have a strong effect on the central endocrine system when administered over three weeks. The concomitant rise in both thyroid hormone and thyroid stimulating hormone is not compatible with normal physiology (which would predict a rise in thyroid hormone with a compensatory decrease in thyroid stimulating hormone or an increase in thyroid stimulating hormone in response to low thyroid hormone).

HEALTH AND WELL-BEING

Rats that inhale bergamot essential oil have been shown to have a decrease in immobility time, which indicates greater motivation and drive, but there was no change in the stress hormone ACTH. In another rat study, animals who inhaled 1% or 2.5% bergamot essential oil were also more likely to move around their cages, and more likely to explore their environment (a marker for reduced stress). 2.5% bergamot essential oil was also shown to inhibit the corticosterone response in animals exposed to a stressful environment (elevated maze).

In mice who had been exposed to unpredictable mild stress, geraniol (a component of rose, ginger, lemon, orange, lavender and other essential oils) reduced the frequency of certain inflammatory markers in the brain that can lead to depression-like behaviors. In a similar test where mice were exposed to mild stress, the essential oil of wild ginger was shown to decrease the expression of the stress hormone precursor corticotropin releasing factor and the enzyme tyrosine hydroxylase that is responsible for the production of l-DOPA (a precursor for both dopamine and epinephrine and nor-epinephrine), and it can prevent the fall of serotonin associated with mild stress.

In a study of healthy, post-menopausal Korean women who inhaled clary sage, serotonin levels significantly increased and cortisol levels significantly decreased. While these women did not have a diagnosis of nor were they being treated for depression, they were screened on a depression scale and split into two groups: one that was more prone to occasional sadness and another that was not. In the group that was more prone to occasional sadness, it was found that cortisol decreased significantly more than in the group that was less prone to occasional sadness.

It is well known that stress can disrupt skin barrier function, and the following study examined rat and human response to stress. The rats subjected to stress who inhaled rose essential oil did not experience the rise in cortisol normally associated with stress, both rats and humans had decreased transepidermal water loss (an index of barrier dysfunction), and humans had a lowered amount of cortisol in the saliva. These findings indicate that rose essential oil can possibly exert action on the hypothalamic-pituitary axis and help mammals respond less robustly to stress.

In mice that were restrained and forcibly exposed to stress, propolis essential oil reduced anxiety-related behaviors and decreased cortisol, ACTH, and malondialdehyde, while increasing the level of superoxide dismutase. These findings suggest that propolis essential oil can impact the function of hypothalamic-pituitary-adrenal axis during times of stress.

In rats subjected to a forced swim test, 5% clary sage reduced stress through modulation of serotonin and dopamine receptors.

Ginger essential oil failed to have a clear impact on mobility and sugar intake in rats under chronic mild stress, but did reduce serum gastrin levels and cholecystokinin in the gut. When combined with magnolia bark extract (which on its own increased serotonin levels and improves mobility and sugar consumption), the combination of effects demonstrates the clinical application of ginger essential oil and magnolia bark extract's paired use in traditional Chinese medicine to alleviate occasional sadness.

In a study of 26 female high school students, girls that wore a necklace diffuser containing an undisclosed essential oil were found to have less daily stress than students who did not wear the necklace. Authors concluded that simply wearing an aroma could be a way to combat normal, daily stress.

In another test of healthy students, 16 people were asked to take a math test and it was found that the levels of chromogranin A (a stress marker) in the saliva lowered significantly 10 minutes after the test when students were exposed to the aroma of lavender oil during the test, but there was no change in cortisol between the test and the control group.

Very young infants given a bath in lavender essential oil-scented baths were found to look at their mothers more, cry less, and spend more time in deep sleep after a bath. Mothers appeared more relaxed, smiled, and touched their infants more in the bath. Both the mothers and the infants had much lower levels of cortisol compared to very young infants and mothers who were given or administered a bath without lavender scent. (Aww, that's sweet).

After five minutes spent inhaling lavender and rosemary essential oil, twenty-two healthy people had decreased levels of cortisol in saliva after and free radical scavenging activities were found to be higher.

Following a two-week long exposure to lemon essential oil, both male and female rats were found to spend more time in the open arms of a maze (a marker of decreased stress), to have lower concentrations of corticosterone, had higher pain thresholds to pain on the paws, and females had decreased pain associated with injection of formalin.

ADVERSE HORMONAL EFFECTS
There is a lengthy discussion in the special populations section about the risk (or lack thereof) that lavender or tea tree oil can cause breast swelling in young boys.

In another study of female rats, a uterotrophic assay (the gold standard test for assessing estrogenic effects of substances) confirmed that topical exposure to 20 and 100 mg/kg of lavender oil in corn oil did not produce any estrogenic effect.

CONCLUSION
As stated above, the answer to this question could go on for much longer. It honestly could be a book on its very own.

#27

WHAT IS THE SAFEST CARRIER OIL FOR SOMEONE WITH NUT ALLERGIES?

SWEET ALMOND
Prunus amygdalus dulcis

Short Answer

In general, people who are allergic to nuts should avoid nut oils, but the risk of cross-reactivity does not necessarily extend to non-tree nuts such as legumes, fruits, and seeds.

Long Answer

If you are allergic to nuts and are concerned about whether or not you might react to a carrier oil, it is important to differentiate between tree nuts (such as almonds, walnuts, pistachios, etc.), legumes (peanuts and soybeans), and seeds (sunflower and sesame) as cross-allergenicity is not the same across each of these classes of plants. The Food Allergy Research and Education group recommends against consumption of any tree nut-containing product, including consumption of tree nut oils, by people who have tree nut allergies. There is no recommendation about topical application; however, it could theoretically be a risk.

Though coconut is sometimes considered a tree nut, it is a fruit, and data shows that the risk of allergenicity in people with tree nut allergies is markedly lower than with wheat, milk, peanut or soy; the risk of cross-allergenicity with other tree nuts is not well-defined. Therefore, many people with tree nut allergies still choose to use coconut oil. Other non-tree nut oils that may interact are beechnut, ginkgo, shea nut, butternut, hickory, chinquapin, lychee nut, pili nut, but the risk is not quantified; therefore, some people with tree nut allergies may respond fine to these ingredients.

People who are allergic to legumes in the Fabaceae family (peanuts and soybeans) may also be allergic to oils derived from these plants, but this does not necessarily extend to the tree nuts. The same logic is true for seeds, where a person who is allergic to sunflower seeds may also be allergic to sunflower seed oil, but the risk does not extend to tree or legume oils.

There is no definitive answer to this question. As with essential oils, if you are not accustomed to the carrier oil, you may consider a patch test prior to first use. If an allergic reaction occurs, consider a carrier oil from another family of plants (tree, seed, or legume). Check labels carefully to ensure that there is not a small amount of carrier oil included in an essential oil blend.

#28

CAN YOU DEVELOP A TOLERANCE OR IMMUNITY TO ESSENTIAL OILS?

CAMPHOR WOOD
Cinnamomum camphora CT linalool

Short Answer

While many people report variable responses to essential oils over time, there is not a well-defined scientific reason why this takes place. Bottom line, if you notice a change in the way your body responds to an essential oil, switch to an essential oil with similar properties and retry with the original oil after a few days or weeks.

Long Answer

In terms of pharmacology, tolerance is a term that means after repeated exposure to a substance, it takes more and more of a substance to produce the same effect. Tolerance does not necessarily indicate addiction, though many substances that are addicting are also associated with tolerance. This is distinctly different than a baseline sensitivity to essential oils, which is more dependent on sensitivity of the skin, lungs, or emotional response to essential oils. Technically speaking, there are no essential oils that lead to tolerance in the former definition.

A search of Google, Google Scholar, and PubMed produced no meaningful results for the "essential oil tolerance." "Tolerance" led to articles regarding initial application, the phrase "oil memory" was not found, and I was instead routed to articles about memory and essential oils. "Frequency fatigue" led to articles about low and high frequency muscle fatigue associated with exercise. I then did what any good scientist would do, and polled the Facebook audience for help.

I then came across the phrase "receptor recycling." This is a process by which nutrient and signaling receptors can be transported from the surface of the cell where they then bind a to protein ligand and proceed to move inside the cell. Once the receptor has given its protein ligand to the target, it can be recycled back up to the cell surface. In the case of nutrient receptors, the process of recycling is quite fast, but it is slower in signaling receptors because excessive stimulation of signaling receptors could be harmful for the body (as is the case in over excitability of epinephrine receptors in heart failure). The recycling of the two different types of receptors is not the same, and a different scaffolding structure holds the receptor under the cell surface before releasing. There are some authors who assume that since there is no evidence that essential oils destroy cell receptors, that they must participate in receptor recycling, and that this is the probable cause of varying responses to essential oils over time, but I have seen no data to prove this.

Even though there is not a well-defined rationale, people do still report varying responses to essential oils over time. Essential oils may become less effective after multiple exposures. There is no defined time, and each person will have a unique response and timeline. A break from the essential oil may help it return to its original level of effectiveness. If you notice an essential oil that you love is not working as well anymore, simply switch to another essential oil with similar properties. Mix up lemon with lime or tangerine, lavender with cedarwood or vetiver, or frankincense with palo santo or elemi. After a few days or weeks, you may try the original essential oil again and see if it returns to the effectiveness that you remember.

#29

IF YOU ARE ALLERGIC TO A PLANT, ARE YOU ALLERGIC TO THE ESSENTIAL OIL OF THAT SAME PLANT?

MANUKA
Leptospermum scoparium

Short Answer

While the incidence of cross reactivity is not well defined, there is a potential risk of cross-allergenicity between essential oils and plants as some of the plant compounds likely responsible for allergy may also be found in essential oils.

Long Answer

There are potentially allergenic chemical constituents in plants that are also found in essential oils. For example, terpenes can be transformed from pre-haptens into haptens and then bind with skin proteins and produce an allergic reaction. Additionally, sensitivity to citrus fruits has been potentially linked to geraniol, citral, and the hydroxyperoxide version of d-limonene. Furthermore, there are a wide variety of sesquiterpene lactones in plants that can react to create allergic reactions, and some of these sesquiterpene lactones may also be present in essential oil. Given that these chemical constituents occur in essential oils, there may be a risk of cross-reaction.

Even though the essential oil may be present in both the plant or pollen, it does not necessarily indicate that a reaction will occur. For example, in a study comparing IgE response to allergens, extracts from the pollen of *C. scoparius L* produced a much more robust reaction than flower extracts of the same plant, and the reactivity of the flower extracts decreased with age of the plants.

Interestingly, sometimes an allergy to one plant may confer cross-reactivity to another. For example, a person who experienced anaphylaxis after ingestion of pine nut showed cross reactivity to mugwort on a skin-prick test. Similarly, a florist with a sunflower allergy also had sensitivity to mugwort and tarragon on a skin prick test. However, it is important to note that mugwort is known to very commonly cause skin reactions, and is not typically sold as an essential oil (though it can be).

If you are allergic to a plant and would like to try the essential oil of the same plant, use caution up front. Use a small amount of the essential oil in a carrier oil on the forearm to complete a patch test, or diffuse a very small amount in an ultra-sonicating diffuser. It is not recommended to ingest the essential oil until you have determined that your skin does not react.

Disease State Interactions

There is much conflicting information about the safety of essential oils for people with diseases, so that is the focus of this section. There are some potential interactions between disease states and essential oils, and if you choose to use essential oils while having a disease, it is imperative that you know how to monitor the disease. (For example, if you have high blood pressure, you should know how to measure your blood pressure.)

#30

CAN ESSENTIAL OILS BE USED IN PEOPLE WITH CONTACT OR ALLERGIC DERMATITIS?

SAGE
Salvia officinalis

Short Answer

Yes, they can; however, the risk of skin reactions may be higher, especially if the person is under stress when they apply the essential oil.

Long Answer

People with contact or allergic dermatitis may be more sensitive to essential oils than people without dermatitis. While allergies to pure essential oils are exceedingly rare and more likely to occur with synthetic constituents of essential oil, reactions may still occur, especially for people with sensitive skin or dermatitis. Before starting with an essential oil, people with dermatitis should consider a patch test. You may also consider dilution, especially with essential oils that are more prone to cause skin irritation such as oregano, clove, cinnamon, cassia, jasmine, lemongrass, basil, and sage.

Even if there is no diagnosis of contact or allergic dermatitis, there is a large minority of people who simply have sensitive skin, especially to cosmetic products. People with sensitive skin may react to ingredients in cosmetics, even those that are not typically classified as irritants. The reactions are not immunological in origin, but simply an intolerance to stimuli that are normally tolerated well by most people.

Interestingly, psychological stress plays an important role in both irritant contact dermatitis and skin sensitivity. That is because the function of the lipids in the stratum corneum is susceptible to increases in psychological stress, and a small reaction may turn into a big reaction because of stress. Stress also reduces skin barrier integrity by increasing the reaction of glucocorticoids. It can prime the immune system for a response and increase the magnitude to which a person responds to a hapten, releasing substance P from nerve endings on the skin and triggering the release of inflammatory cytokines from mast cells. While there is no direct data to lead to this conclusion, it is reasonable to assume that reactions may be exaggerated if there is a heightened sense of stress related to the use of the essential oil, cosmetic, or product. Therefore, it is important that people with contact or allergic dermatitis use essential oils that they feel comfortable with, and avoid using essential oils that cause feelings of stress within them.

Weather may also play a role in skin sensitivity, and you may find that your skin is more likely to react during certain times of the year versus others. Dermatitis may worsen during cold and dry weather seasons, and additional moisturizer may help to alleviate some of the symptoms and increase the tolerability of essential oils.

Skin ailments, especially dermatitis, are often linked to the diet, and up to 40% of skin reactions may have their origin in food. Be sure that your diet is full of foods, not food-like products that are full of artificial ingredients.

As with almost any disease state, essential oils can be used in people with contact or allergic dermatitis with proper precautions such as patch testing, dilution, and a big dose of confidence.

#31

WHY IS THERE A WARNING FOR BASIL ESSENTIAL OIL FOR USE IN PEOPLE WITH SEIZURES?

BASIL
Ocimum basilicum

Short Answer

Basil essential oil interacts with certain medicines used to treat epilepsy.

Long Answer

Epilepsy is a disorder where brain neuron activity is abnormal. It may exhibit symptoms as mild as blank stares to as severe as tonic-clonic seizures where the person loses consciousness and flails his or her arms and legs. Though widely purported online as contraindicated for use in epilepsy, there are no precautions or contraindications to basil for patients with epilepsy or seizure mentioned in the Natural Standard or in Natural Medications database. Additionally, basil was used in many traditional and cultural medication remedies for epilepsy, and studies suggest that basil may be safe for use in patients with epilepsy. Two common varieties of basil are *Ocimum basilicum* (sweet basil, more common) and *Ocimum sanctum* (holy basil).

The mechanism for why basil may affect abnormal brain activity is not fully understood. Holy basil extract has been shown to decrease convulsive activity in electroshock models. Eugenol extracted from sweet basil has also been shown to decrease action potential in nerves in animal models. Preliminary research indicates that basil may help to alleviate mental fatigue and increase alertness while simultaneously decreasing anxiety. Studies of basil, basil extract, and basil oils have demonstrated anti-inflammatory, anti-oxidant, and neuroprotective properties.

Basil essential oil interacts with barbiturate medications including phenobarbital, pentobarbital, and secobarbital. The person may experience increased lethargy and sedation if both basil essential oil and barbiturates are used. Use of diazepam for seizures or anxiety may cause amnesia, and basil essential oil may lessen amnesia. Data regarding the combination of other medications used for epilepsy and basil are lacking.

Basil essential oil should be used with caution in patients with hypothyroidism as it has been shown to decrease blood levels of thyroid hormone (T4). Basil may also inhibit sperm production, act as a topical spermicidal agent, and inhibit fertility, and should be used with caution by people who wish to become pregnant. Basil may lower blood pressure, thin blood, lower cholesterol, or lower blood sugar, and caution should be used in patients who take blood pressure medications, blood thinners (anticoagulants or antiplatelets), anti-diabetic, or cholesterol reducing medications.

#32

CAN PEOPLE WITH DIABETES USE ESSENTIAL OILS?

OCOTEA
Ocotea quixos

— *Short Answer* —

While a body of evidence supports the notion that foods containing polyphenols can be useful in preventing and treating diabetes, there is no robust human data to suggest that the support for the endocrine system extends to essential oils. Essential oil aromas may play a role in creating a relaxing environment when performing blood sugar checks, and proprietary blends of essential and fatty oils may help to reduce pain associated with diabetic neuropathy. If you choose to use essential oils and have a diagnosis of diabetes, I encourage you to check your blood sugar at least three times per day or more.

Long Answer

There is a growing body of evidence inferring that polyphenols in food such as green tea, pomegranates, berries, cinnamon, grapes, chocolate, and olive oil may aid in the prevention and management of type 2 diabetes. The proposed action of food-based polyphenols is that they inhibit α-amylase, α-glucosidase and inhibit the gut glucose transporter of sodium-dependent glucose transporter 1 (SGLT1). These mechanisms reduce hepatic glucose output and increase the rate of insulin-dependent glucose uptake. Though constituents of essential oils have been shown in vitro and in animals to duplicate some of these mechanisms, there is no robust human data that essential oils can mimic the actions of food-based polyphenols. Furthermore, much of the data related to essential oils is in drug-induced animal models of diabetes, and it is unknown exactly how this will relate to diabetes in humans.

In this section, we review in vitro data. African cardamom and grains of paradise essential oils are high in eugenol, eucalyptol, α-terpineol, α-caryophyllene, and β-caryophyllene. Both essential oils were found to inhibit α-amylase, α-glucosidase, and angiotensin-I-converting enzyme (ACE) in vitro. In another in vitro study of rat pancreas, clove bud essential oil (high in α-pinene, β-pinene, neral, geranial, gamma terpinene, cis-ocimene, allo-ocimene, 1,8-cineole, linalool, borneol, myrcene and pinene-2-ol) inhibited α-amylase and α-glucosidase in a dose-dependent manner, and it exhibited antioxidant activity. Certain plants traditionally used for diabetes such as *Myrcia uniflora* species have been show in vitro to inhibit thyroid function and may lead to hypothyroidism when combined with iodine deficiency. In an in vitro study, Ashanti black pepper essential oil decreased the activity of α-amylase, α-glucosidase, and ACE. These studies suggest that additional research is needed to determine the effects of essential oils in people with diabetes.

In this section, we review animal models with drug-induced diabetes. In a study of rats with streptyzocin- or alloxan-induced diabetes, essential oil of the *Zygophyllum album L* inhibited α-amylase, which dropped blood sugar by 60% and hemoglobin A1C by 17%. The results of another similar study showed a drop in fasting blood sugar as well as an increase in liver levels of glycogen. In another animal study with drug-induced diabetes, the isolated essential oil constituent trans-anethole decreased blood sugar and hemoglobin A1C. In a third study of drug-induced diabetes, oral administration of *Melissa officinalis* essential oil restored blood glucose back to normal and reduced body weight. Pretreatment with a rare species of lavender (*L. stoechas*) protected against the rise in blood sugar associated with alloxan, and the protection was at least partially attributed to antioxidant properties.

Another interesting take on the role of essential oils in people with diabetes is the offsetting of side effects. In children with type 1 diabetes, diffusing lavender and orange in the room decreased the change in heart rate associated with painful stimuli, but it did not decrease the perception of pain.

Though studies are not well-defined, certain essential oils may interact with select anti-diabetic medicines and produce either hyper- or hypoglycemia. If you are using metformin, glibenclamide, or tolbutamide for diabetes, use caution with anise, black seed, cumin, cinnamon bark, fennel, fenugreek, geranium, lemongrass, marjoram, may chang, Melissa, myrtle, oregano, savory, tea tree, thyme, turmeric, and verbena.

If you choose to use essential oils with diabetes, and especially when taking anti-diabetic medicines, it is important that you check your blood sugar regularly, at least three times per day or more. At a minimum, it is suggested to check your fasting blood sugar first thing in the morning, and two hours after the largest meal of the day. If you notice an increase or decrease in your blood sugar or notice any signs of hypoglycemia (low blood sugar: dizziness, tiredness, hunger, irritation, etc.) or hyperglycemia (high blood sugar: thirst, excessive urination, weight loss, blurry vision, etc.), talk to a health care professional who is skilled in the use of essential oils.

#33

CAN PEOPLE WITH LUNG DISEASE USE ESSENTIAL OILS?

NUTMEG
Myristica fragrans

--- *Short Answer* ---

Yes, if you choose to. Essential oils have a very low likelihood of causing respiratory disease, but occasionally may cause reactions in people with disease when oils are inhaled at moderate to high concentrations over an extended period. The risk of irritation or reaction is lower with essential oils than with perfumes.

Long Answer

Volatile organic compounds (VOCs) may cause lung irritation whether there is a history of lung disease or not. VOCs are defined as any compound of carbon (excluding carbon monoxide, carbon dioxide, carbonic acid, metallic carbides or carbonates and ammonium carbonate) which participates in atmospheric photochemical reactions, except those designated by the EPA as having negligible photochemical reactivity. These include substances such as chloroform, formaldehyde, benzene, toluene, perfumes, and essential oils. Reactions may be respiratory but may not necessarily be. For example, consistent use of air fresheners and aerosols can increase diarrhea in infants and headaches in new mothers. Very few essential oils have been implicated in provoking respiratory responses, especially compared to substances like chlorine or formaldehyde; however, long-term exposure to mixtures of terpenes may carry a health risk.

Adverse respiratory effects of airborne substances may be subdivided into sensory irritation and bronchial hyper-reactivity, and further credence must be given to people who have respiratory disease at the baseline, such as asthma and chronic obstructive pulmonary disease (COPD).

When considering a potential sensory irritation, it is important to look at the concentration of the molecule required to provide a response. In mice, chlorine and formaldehyde each produce a 50% decrease in respiratory rate (RD_{50}) at a concentration of 3.5-4 ppm. This was used to calculate a more conservative estimate of when lung irritation may occur (0.03 X RD_{50}), yielding a calculated irritation threshold of 0.1 ppm. Rare constituents of essential oils such as 1-Octen-3-ol, 3-Octanol, and Benzaldehyde have a calculated irritation threshold of

1-11 ppm (10-100 times higher concentration than chlorine/formaldehyde). More common essential oils constituents such as limonene, α and β-pinene, δ-3-carene, and menthol require concentrations of 30-50 ppm (300-500 times higher than the concentration of chlorine/formaldehyde). Other constituents require even higher concentrations to produce irritation, whereas constituents are not irritants at all (vanillin, octanoic acid, coumarin, for example).

Respiratory sensory irritation is distinctly different than an olfactory response, as a respiratory sensory irritation is not triggered by olfaction nor is it dependent on an aroma. Sensory irritation occurs when an odorant molecule activates the trigeminal nerve in the nose, mouth and eyes. As opposed to an interpretation system for aromas, this system acts as a warning system against potentially hazardous chemicals. The reactions can be multiplicative with responses varying from irritation, burning, tickling, warming, cooling, in nasal and oral cavities, and cornea in the eye. Psychology may influence the perception and reporting of sensory irritation. This was demonstrated in a study where two groups of people were asked to inhale methyl salicylate. One group was told that the substance was a natural product and the other group was told that it was an industrial cleaner, and the latter group reported 5-10x the intensity of nose, throat, and eye irritation.

Oxidation of essential oil terpenes can follow exposure to oxygen or ozone, and oxidative by-products may cause sensory irritation. α-pinene, β-pinene, camphene, ϱ-cymene, and (+)-limonene have all been shown to react with airborne ozone at levels below observable effect level. However, it is unknown what effect these by-products may have on daily life. In mice, exposure to a combination of 0.05 ppm ozone and 35 ppm (+)-limonene for 35 minutes reduced respiratory rate by up day, though the duration and essential oils were not described. Neither the Global Initiative for Chronic Obstructive Lung Disease (GOLD) guidelines, The American Thoracic Society guidelines, nor the National Institute for Health and Care Excellence (NICE) make mention of essential oils, so there is no guidance on whether to use. This is a clear situation of "you may use them if you choose to."

Asthma is characterized by repeated, reversible symptoms of airway obstruction. Asthma taking place during working hours is exceedingly rare due to inhalation of essential oils. In fact, a database of more than 300 substances that may cause asthma does not list any essential oils, and only lists three essential oil constituents (carene, (+)-limonene and styrene); however, turpentine vapors (containing (+)-limonene and δ-3-carene) has caused occupational asthma in two people (however one also inhaled rosin which also may have contributed to the reaction).

Most asthma is allergenic, not irritant, and essential oils have never been implicated as a cause of irritant asthma; however, one case report has noted new onset allergic asthma following inhalation of menthol (though this is contrary to additional data that suggests menthol may help to tone down airway excitability). Allergic asthma is a result of increased inflammatory mediators such as leukotrienes, cytokines, TNF-α, and histamine, and certain essential oils constituents such as chamazulene, bergapten, eugenol, α-humulene, β-carophyllene, as well as whole lavender, ajowan and cedarwood oil have been shown to modulate the inflammatory process and reduce inflammatory mediators. Furthermore, Tisserand and Yee report that there was no literature suggesting an exacerbation of asthma symptoms from essential oils, but that seven people with asthma responded to an online call and stated that they had sensitivities to essential oils. All reported that they were more sensitive to commercial fragrances than essential oils.

Be sure to take caution when instilling essential oils in the noses of infants as serious reactions such as wheezing, cyanosis, and respiratory collapse have been reported. Accidental administration of menthol and 1,8-cineole in nasal preparations has been shown to cause respiratory distress in children less than 4 years old. If you choose to use these essential oils on your young child, use additional caution and consider very strong dilution or avoidance of the face and nose.

Essential oils rarely cause eye and airway irritation, and the most commonly reported molecules are monoterpenes (pinenes, carenes, limonenes). If someone is very sensitive to aromas, you may consider minimizing exposure to these. Essential oils have not been shown to cause respiratory diseases, though fragrance molecules carry a small risk of irritation in areas with high concentrations of ozone, and in people with preexisting disease. If you choose to use essential oils and have a diagnosis of respiratory disease, "start low and go slow," and ensure that the aromas are tolerable. You may consider dilution before applying to the skin or diffusion of a small amount in a large, ventilated room.

Recently, rumors have been going around that essential oils can accumulate in the lungs, even to the point of being seen on bronchoscopy. Select pulmonologists have educated people (even those without lung disease) to stop using essential oils in diffusers in response. To this I respond with a resounding "no." I reviewed dozens of articles of case reports of lipid (or lipoid) pneumonia, and none reported essential oils as a cause. References reveal that ingested cod liver oil, ingested

#34

SHOULD PEOPLE WITH AUTOIMMUNE DISEASES USE ESSENTIAL OILS?

ORANGE
Citrus aurantium dulcis

--- *Short Answer* ---

You can if you choose to use them. There is virtually no data to make an evidence-based decision in favor or against.

Long Answer

There is virtually no data to make an evidence-based decision in favor of or against the use of essential oils for autoimmune disease. There is some in vitro and animal data that suggests that essential oils and their constituents can impact inflammatory mediators such as T-cells and T helper cells, but there is little to no evidence in humans that they are either harmful or beneficial.

For example, essential oil from the Brazil legume *Pterodon polygalaeflorus* has been shown to arrest cell cycle and decrease the number of several subtypes of T cells in vitro. In a rat model of drug-induced rheumatoid arthritis, turmeric essential oil injected into the belly was found to be effective at reducing join inflammation, but (possibly due to the high dose of 56 mg/kg/day; roughly equivalent to 65 drops per day in an adult) was also found to be toxic. Ingesting a 20-fold higher amount was non-toxic and reduced joint inflammation by 20%.

In another study of drug-induced rheumatoid arthritis in rats, black seed oil extract (high in thymoquine) suppressed symptoms such as claw inflammation (and this was confirmed on X-ray) and decreased levels of TNF-alpha and IL-1 beta, but this study was retracted for unknown reason and therefore cannot be used to guide decisions.

There is data showing that terpinen-4-ol may help to support the appearance of skin, even in people with psoriasis, and additional evidence suggests that aromatherapy can support well-being.

The more I researched the question of autoimmune disorders, the more I found articles regarding diet as treatment instead of essential oils. For example, in humans, fatty oils of hemp seed and evening primrose, alone and alongside a hot-nature diet, have been shown to improve the symptoms of relapsing-remitting multiple sclerosis. A review article of evening primrose oil and borage oil confirmed that data paints a positive picture for using the oils with rheumatic conditions, and authors contend that it is likely due to the essential fatty acids that shift away from arachidonic acid (a pro-inflammatory food component). Another review article contends that the more omega-3 fatty acids we can consume (from flax and hemp seed oils or fish) and the fewer omega-6 fatty acids (from poultry, eggs, cereal, grapeseed and canola oil), the more likely we are to be able to control autoimmune disorders. This is a bit confusing since evening primrose oil is more than 75% linoleic acid and 10% gamma linoleic acid, an omega-6. Further review suggests that both omega-3s and omega-6s are preferable to saturated fats, and that the Western diet (which is high in saturated fats) may lead to a functional deficiency in essential fatty acids that leads to various autoimmune disorders including multiple sclerosis, Sjögren's syndrome, and cardiovascular disease.

While there is no data to suggest that essential oils can be helpful in people with autoimmune disease, there is no data to suggest that they are harmful either. What is well known is that essential fatty acids are critical in both the prevention and treatment of autoimmune diseases including type 1 diabetes, multiple sclerosis, and Sjögren's syndrome. With autoimmune disorders, I suggest focusing more on the dietary origins than on the use of essential oils.

#35

SHOULD PEPPERMINT ESSENTIAL OIL BE AVOIDED IN PEOPLE WITH HEARTBURN?

PEPPERMINT
Mentha piperita

Short Answer

Some people who have heartburn or GERD symptoms are sensitive to peppermint while others are not. A search for studies on the matter revealed relatively little.

Long Answer

People with heartburn or gastrointestinal reflux disease (GERD) may suffer from occasional dyspepsia (indigestion). GERD is caused when stomach acids rise past the lower esophageal sphincter and reflux into the esophagus. Symptoms include burning in the chest and throat, chest pain, difficulty swallowing, dry cough, hoarseness or sore throat, regurgitation of food or sour liquid, or a lump in the back of the throat. Risk factors for GERD include being overweight, wearing clothing that is too tight, pregnancy, smoking, asthma, diabetes, hiatal hernia, dry mouth, connective tissue disorders, and delayed stomach emptying. There are a wide variety of medicines to treat GERD, and it is very important to also follow the lifestyle recommendations.

Peppermint is often included in lists of foods that should be avoided in people with GERD symptoms. Peppermint oil is known to relax the lower esophageal sphincter, theoretically making it more likely that gastric contents will reflux in to the esophagus. A PubMed database search for "peppermint oil and heartburn" revealed three results all on the topic of irritable bowel syndrome, not heartburn. A search for "peppermint oil and GERD" revealed two results, neither of which was applicable to the subject under question.

Therefore, I expanded the search to exclude the word "oil" and found that studies conclude that daily consumption of peppermint tea can increase the symptoms of GERD. In a review article, authors suggest that neither spearmint nor peppermint improve or worsen symptoms, but that peppermint oil can speed the first phase of gastric emptying, increase relaxation time of the pyloric valve, and decrease resting esophageal sphincter pressure. The authors further suggest that peppermint and peppermint oil may be distinctly different, and as a result, support gastrointestinal health differently.

Based on the available information, it is my professional opinion that there is a lack of evidence that peppermint essential oil should always be avoiding in people with GERD; however, if you find that it aggravates your condition, you may choose to avoid ingesting peppermint essential oil.

Long Answer

Certain essential oils contain molecules that may mimic natural estrogens. Whole essential oils have been studied in vitro, and fennel and anise have been shown to have estrogenic activity, whereas bay, cinnamon bark, clove, dill, orange, pimento, and thyme essential oils had no effect.

Clary sage essential oil contains approximately 4% sclareol, which (if you really squint) is somewhat structurally similar to estradiol; however, studies have shown that sclareol is unlikely to have estrogen-mimicking effects due to its structure. An isomer of sclareol (13-epi-sclareol) has been shown to possibly interact with the estrogen receptor, and the study suggests that it may inhibit estrogen receptors. This does not imply that clary sage cannot provide support to women of all ages, it just may not be for interactions with the estrogen receptor. While the use of clary sage essential oil following estrogen-linked cancer is the topic of much internet debate, it does not seem that the rationale is always appropriate. One thing is for sure, clary sage will not give you cancer, but, if you choose to be very conservative, you may choose to avoid it if you have had an estrogen-linked cancer.

Chemical constituents of oils have been assessed in vitro, and (E)-anethole has appeared to have weak estrogenic activity in multiple studies. This suggests necessary caution when using fennel (sweet or bitter), anise, or star anise essential oil. In vitro studies have shown that citral, geraniol, nerol, and eugenol can displace estrogen from receptors at very high concentrations, with all but eugenol activating the receptor and eugenol inhibiting the receptor. Massive doses of bergepten and methoxsalen enhanced the metabolism of estrogens, altered ovarian follicle function, and ovulation; however, the dose was so large it is unlikely to have any bearing on occasional use of essential oils that are high in these compounds.

An article suggested that lavender and tea tree oils can cause breast swelling in young boys, but an in-depth review of this article leads me to believe that it is not accurate and should not lead anyone to the conclusion that they are estrogenic (see Question 46).

It may be reasonable to avoid fennel, anise and star anise if you have had an estrogen-linked cancer, and ultimately the decision is yours. If you want to be extra conservative, you may also avoid clary sage. Tea tree and lavender oils should have never been included as risky for inducing estrogenic activity, and I do not think it is necessary to avoid them unless you want to be extraordinarily cautious (arguably for no good reason).

#37

CAN PEOPLE WITH HYPERTENSION USE ESSENTIAL OILS?

CYPRESS
Cupressus sempervirens

Short Answer

Yes. There is conflicting information online about safety regarding certain essential oils that may be outdated at this point. It is very important that you know the signs and symptoms of both high and low blood pressure if you have hypertension or are taking antihypertensive medicines.

Long Answer

There is information online that people with hypertension (high blood pressure) should not use certain essential oils (rosemary, hyssop, sage and thyme for example), and this is primarily based on the publication of "Aromathérapie" by Jean Valnet in 1964. This text cites two authors that are said to support the argument that these essential oils raise blood pressure: Caujolle and Cazal. The Caujolle study citation appears to be errant, as the paper Valnet cites concludes that lavender, lavandin, and spike lavender all reduce blood pressure following intravenous administration in dogs. So, we disregard this piece of data; the Cazal study has been lost throughout history.

Let's explore the data that we have. In one study, dogs were given an infusion of 1-3 mL of a "saturated solution" of hyssop essential oil in 33°F alcohol (brrrrrr…), which resulted in a brief decrease in blood pressure followed by a rapid rise in blood pressure at the onset on convulsions. This is just one example of how blood pressure and the onset of convulsions are related in literature about essential oils. It does appear that it is possible to raise blood pressure when enough essential oil is injected to induce seizures (which hopefully you are not doing). Other studies confirm that convulsant-inducing injections of essential oils may raise blood pressure in cats and dogs, while in studies of normotensive animals, 1,8-cineole, α-terpinole, nerol, geraniol, citronellol, and linalool all decreased blood pressure.

In vivo and in vitro studies have demonstrated that menthol has calcium channel-blocking effects, and it reduces local blood pressure when applied topically. Other studies suggest similar calcium channel-blocking effects from thymol, carvacrol, cinnamaldehyde, and papaverine. While it is unknown what effect this will have on humans, the calcium channel-blocking effects make it unlikely that these essential oils constituents can induce hypertension.

Human data is inconclusive. In two studies of normotensive people, both cold-pressed garlic oil and steam distilled garlic oil decreased both systolic and diastolic blood pressure when given at approximately 18 mg/day for 4-16 weeks. Temporary increases in blood pressure are documented after intensive, intentional inhalation of grapefruit, black pepper, fennel, or tarragon oil for more than three to seven minutes. In healthy people, ylang ylang and cedrol appear to lower blood pressure. Some studies conclude that lavender may lower blood pressure, whereas others show no effect following inhalation.

Authors have further tried to delineate whether changes in blood pressure are due to physiological or psychological factors, as both tend to come into play. Physiologically, when injected intravenously some essential oils directly act on calcium channels. When inhaled, effects may be autonomically mediated with changes in the sympathetic and parasympathetic nervous system coming into play. One study concluded that ingested fenugreek oil can inhibit angiotensin-converting enzyme. Therefore, it is possible that the route of administration has a big impact on the outcome of the study.

Tisserand concludes: "Eucalyptus, camphor, pine, thyme, and peppermint oils should be scratched from cautionary lists. Hyssop and sage essential oils are only a risk in convulsant oral doses, and lower doses are very likely to be hypotensive. It is likely that rosemary oil follows the same pattern. Inhalation data suggest that essential oils presenting a risk include grapefruit, lemon, caraway, black pepper, fennel, tarragon and other oils high in carvone or limonene. However, in human studies the increases were only slight."

Given the conflicting information, and the extensive misinformation online related to thyme, hyssop, sage, and rosemary, I suggest that you monitor your blood pressure if you are concerned about hypertension and essential oils. If you choose to use any essential oil with a diagnosis of hypertension or if you take antihypertensive medications, please talk to your doctor and pharmacist about the signs and symptoms of both high and low blood pressure. Some signs of low blood pressure include dizziness or lightheadedness, fainting, lack of concentration, blurred vision, nausea, and fatigue. Some signs of very high blood pressure are blood spots in the eye, facial flushing, and dizziness. Talk to your physician quickly if any of these symptoms occur.

Certain signs of high blood pressure should be immediately reported to a physician. High blood pressure does not usually cause headaches or nosebleeds. If you have a severe headache, nosebleed, severe anxiety, or shortness of breath, and if your blood pressure is above 180/110 mmHg, sit down and relax for five minutes. If symptoms persist, alert a physician immediately. If you have elevated blood pressure greater than 180/120 mmHg along with any sign of end organ damage (loss of consciousness, loss of vision, loss of memory, decreased urine production, chest pain, shortness of breath) or stroke (facial droop, arm weakened, speech difficulties), call your emergency response team immediately.

#38

CAN PEOPLE WHO HAVE HAD A TRANSPLANT USE ESSENTIAL OILS?

RAVINTSARA
Cinnamomum camphora

Short Answer

You can if you choose to use them. There is virtually no data to make an evidence-based decision in favor or against; however, the specific data we have does not demonstrate positive results.

Long Answer

In an assertive letter to the *Journal of Antimicrobial Chemotherapy*, a writer contends that essential oils need to be investigated further in the setting of both cancer and transplant. He maintains that essential oils are known to have anti-inflammatory and cytophylactic (immune-stimulating) effects in vitro, in healthy animals, and in healthy humans, and makes a case based on each of them. For anti-inflammatory properties, such as 1,8-cineole's ability to inhibit cytokine production, he maintains that administration to an immunosuppressed person could presumably further deplete the immune system, potentially leading to infection.

He counters that an the immune-stimulating properties of an essential oil may produce a drug interaction with immunosuppressive medications. He concludes that there needs to be greater discussion before proceeding to use essential oil in oncology or transplant units in the hospital.

I reached out to this author as this letter appears to be a comment on another study, and I was intrigued by what the study may have examined, but the author was not reachable at the email provided on the publication.

There have been studies to test the effectiveness of essential oils for immunocompromised people and their caregivers (to support the extra stress, anxiety and decision making that may accompany treatment for disease, and simply to enhance quality of life), and the data is a mix of both positive and negative. In certain studies, repeated courses are required to glean any positive effects. Nausea is a common side effect of immunosuppressant medicines, and in a study of adults with nausea as a side effect of a medicine, smelling fresh cut oranges was more effective at reducing symptoms than orange essential oil. In children undergoing stem cell transplant, inhalation of bergamot essential oil has been shown to increase anxiety and nausea.

Ultimately, it is up to you if you choose to use essential oils with the medicines required for transplantation. There is a dearth of data on the subject. If you choose to use essential oils around the time of transplant, I encourage you to discuss with your physician and suggest that the experience be published as a case report.

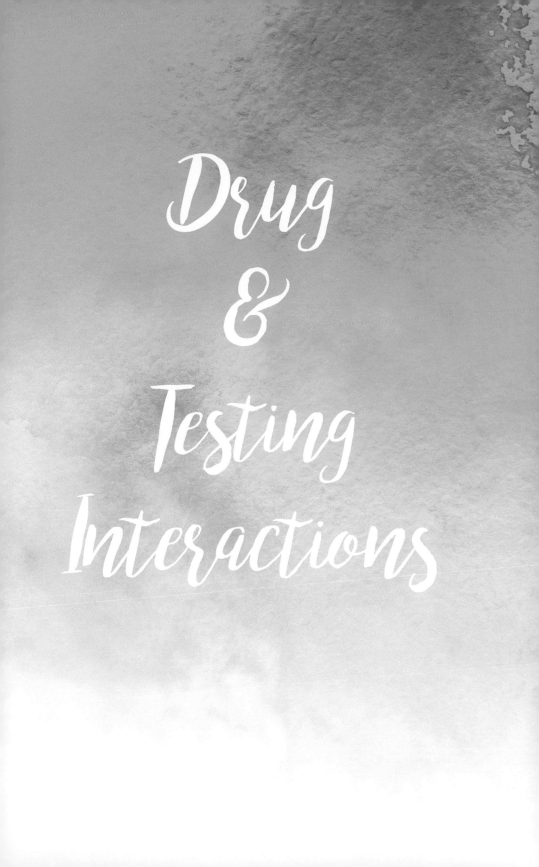

Questions regarding how to best use essential oils alongside medications are some of the most challenging questions to answer, as there is very little human data where whole essential oil has been examined for pharmacokinetic interactions with medications. Another concern is whether essential oils will cause a false positive on a drug test, such as those that may be given to both human and animal athletes. Both questions will be covered in this section.

#39

WHAT ARE DRUG INTERACTIONS AND WHERE DO THEY ARISE?

GERMAN CHAMOMILE
Matricaria recutita

Short Answer

Drug interactions occur when one medicine changes the activity of another when they are administered together. Many drug interactions occur via induction or inhibition of liver enzymes, but may also occur in almost any body system, in the blood, and on the surface of cells.

Long Answer

Drug interactions are defined as when a combination of medications can produce a clinically significant change in the pharmacologic response that is larger or smaller than the sum of the effects when the drugs are administered separately. The variation is related to pharmacokinetics, which is the study of the how much and how fast a foreign substance is absorbed by the body, distributed through the body, metabolized by the body, and eliminated from the body.

All manner of foreign substances, essential oils included, interact with the body, and this may lead to questions about whether certain essential oils should be avoided by people on certain medications, with certain disease states, or with a history of disease. As always, it is advised to consult a health care professional knowledgeable about essential oils and your personal health history before embarking on any new routine.

Let's start with what drug interactions are and how they occur. Many drug interactions arise from the liver. The liver is the most active metabolizing organ in the body, and it is equipped with a plethora of drug metabolizing enzymes that break down medications and foreign substances into execrable metabolites. Enzymes in the liver are known by many names: cytochromes, CYPs (pronounced 'sips'), P450, etc. Furthermore, enzymes may be named specifically (eg. CYP3A4, 1A2, 2C9, etc). CYP function varies in each person based on age, race, and individual genetics.

Metabolism is broken into three types: Phase 1, 2, and 3. Phase 1 is basic chemistry: oxidation, reduction, and hydrolysis. They may be enzyme dependent, such as those in the liver via monooxygenase activity, or they can be enzyme independent and be a byproduct of pH changes such as those that happen in the stomach. Byproducts of phase 1 metabolism may not be immediately excretable and may undergo further transformation in phase 2 metabolism. Additionally, phase 1 metabolism can activate substances (such as prodrugs to active drugs) or toxify substances (where non-toxic starting materials become toxic). Phase 2 metabolism uses an enzyme to add a group to the existing molecule and ensures that the group is water soluble and highly excretable. Groups that can be added include sulfate, methyl, acetyl, glucuronide, glutathione and glycine; and each is enzyme dependent. With conjugation to one of these groups, most of the products are rendered water soluble and not available for further use by the body; however, some may proceed to further phase 3 reactions. These reactions can take place in the liver as well as the kidneys, lungs, central nervous system, intestine, prostate, red blood cells, and more. Phase 3 takes the conjugation products, removes them and then acetylates them and prepares them for excretion.

Many of the processes listed above are dependent on enzyme activity, and many foods and medications can alter the function of enzymes. When we inhibit an enzyme, metabolism of any substrate of that enzyme will decrease (meaning that the medication or foreign substance will stay in the body longer). If we induce the enzyme, metabolism of the substrate will speed up (meaning that the medication or foreign substance does not stay in the body as long). Examples of medications that can induce CYP enzymes include rifampin and carbamazepine, and medications that can inhibit are cimetidine, omeprazole, ritonavir and many more.

Wild mountain sage, brown and yellow camphor, lemongrass, blue chamomile, blue tansy, and yarrow essential oils have been shown in vitro to interact with select cytochromes, and some authors suggest caution with these essential oils even when applied topically. The list of essential oils and essential oil constituents that have been shown to interact with enzymes are too numerous to name here. Plus, I don't want to provide a huge list that would dissuade people on medications from using essential oils, as many of the combinations are possibly incompatible and not demonstrably incompatible. Instead I will again encourage: if you choose to use an essential oil while on a medication, know the signs and symptoms of adverse effects that may indicate your medication level is too high and be quick to discuss them with your health care provider. If you use essential oils while on blood thinners, know the signs and symptoms of bleeding. If you use essential oils while on anti-diabetic medicines, check your blood sugar regularly and know the signs and symptoms of hypo- and hyperglycemia. If you use essential oils while on antidepressants classified as selective serotonin reuptake inhibitors, know the signs and symptoms of serotonin syndrome.

Basically, if you are on a medicine, know your medicine and know your pharmacist. Pharmacists are an excellent resource to teach you about your medicines as they are highly trained in both the science of medicines and how to break science down and make things simple.

Efflux pumps such as P-glycoprotein in the liver, jejunum, colon, pancreas, and kidney effectively pick up foreign substances from the cell and toss them out of the cell in an energy-dependent process. Medications such as proton pump inhibitors, calcium channel blockers, and certain antidepressants can inhibit P-glycoprotein, thereby increasing the duration of time a substrate will stay in the body. The extent to which essential oils can affect drug transport is not clear; however, the effect is likely small.

Many medications are carried in the blood with plasma binding proteins (PBPs), and certain essential oil constituents such as β-elemene, bergapten, (+)-limonene have been shown to bind to plasma proteins. This could lead to a potential displacement of medication from PBPs, making it available both for pharmacologic action and for metabolism and excretion.

At the cellular level, foreign substances can compete with endogenous substance for binding sites on the cell. The essential oil constituent (*E*)-anethole is structurally similar to catecholamines such as dopamine, epinephrine and norepinephrine, and it may compete with these substances for binding sites on cell surfaces.

Lastly there are foreign substances that change the potency of medicines by interacting with their targets. For example, there are many foreign substances that contain high levels of methyl salicylate that may potentiate the action of blood thinners because methyl salicylate directly inhibits platelet function and exacerbates blood thinning. Many authors recommend that those on blood thinners be cautious when using wintergreen essential oil.

Monoamine oxidase (MAO) is an enzyme that breaks down neurotransmitters. Certain anti-depressant medicines and anti-Parkinsonism medicines inhibit this enzyme as a part of their therapeutic action. These medications are generally not first line agents as they have a long slew of side effects. Nevertheless, myristicin and nutmeg essential oils have been shown to inhibit MAO in rat brains, as has eugenol. Avoid overuse of nutmeg and essential oils high in eugenol. While not a drug interaction, certain enzymes such as glucose-6-phosphate dehydrogenase may be deficient in individuals, especially male children of Chinese, West African,

Mediterranean and Middle Eastern descent. In fact, there are more than 140 ways that the genes that encode this enzyme can be altered and lead to varying states of function. A wide variety of medicines lead to increased risk of hemolysis in these patients. Children with G6PD deficiency may be slow to metabolize menthol, and people who lack the enzyme should avoid overuse of essential oils high in menthol.

I reiterate: know your medicine, and know your pharmacist. Be a conscious observer of your body, and look for signs of symptoms of toxicity from medicines.

#40

DOES GRAPEFRUIT ESSENTIAL OIL INTERACT WITH MEDICATIONS?

GRAPEFRUIT
Citrus paradisi

Short Answer

It is very unlikely that grapefruit essential oil interacts with medications in the same manner as grapefruit juice.

Long Answer

Grapefruit juice contains compounds that are potent inhibitors of drug-metabolizing enzymes known as cytochromes. When cytochromes are inhibited, drug levels increase and so does the risk of adverse effects. Medications that may be affected by grapefruit juice include cholesterol-lowering medications known as statins, and certain anti-anxiety, anti-allergy, anti-arrhythmic, antibiotic, anti-hypertensive, anti-retroviral, and erectile dysfunction medications.

The most potent inhibitor of cytochromes found in grapefruit juice is 6,7-dihydroxybergotamottin (DHB); and grapefruit flavonoids, bergamattin and bergapten are less potent inhibitors of cytochromes. DHB is found in high concentrations in grapefruit juice, but not in grapefruit oil. There are other flavonoids such as bergamattin and bergapten that are found in grapefruit oil and other citrus oils; however, they are weak inhibitors (CYP3A4) and the likelihood of them causing clinically important drug interactions is much lower than with 6,7-DHB.

In my professional opinion, grapefruit oil may be used by people who take medications that interact with grapefruit juice; however, it is prudent to know the early signs and symptoms of drug interactions (for example, muscle cramps or weakness in patients on statins). Talk to your pharmacist about what you should look out for.

#41

DO ESSENTIAL OILS INTERACT WITH BLOOD THINNERS?

MARJORAM
Origanum majorana

— *Short Answer* —

It is wise to not overuse wintergreen and other essential oils if you are taking blood thinning medications.

Long Answer

There is no definitive list of essential oils to avoid on blood thinners; however, there are some oils that have either an actual or a theoretical risk of potentiating the action of blood thinners. For example, wintergreen essential oil is comprised of more than 95% methyl salicylate. Methyl salicylate in medications has been well demonstrated to potentiate the action of blood thinning medications including warfarin (Coumadin®), aspirin, and others. In studies where authors conclude that wintergreen essential oil increases the risk of bleeding, they do not differentiate between wintergreen essential oil and synthetic oil of wintergreen. Oil of wintergreen is the most common type of wintergreen oil on the market as it is very easy to synthesize in mass quantities.

Additional essential oils that may interact with anticoagulant (warfarin, enoxaparin (Lovenox®), fondaparinux (Artixtra®), dabigatran (Pradaxa®), apixaban (Eliquis®), rivaroxaban (Xarelto®) etc.) and antiplatelet medicines (aspirin, prasugrel (Effient®), ticagrelor (Brilinta®), ticlopidine (Ticlid®), etc.) include anise, basil, birch, cassia, cinnamon bark, fennel, lavandin, marjoram, myrtle, oregano, patchouli, ravintsara, savory, thyme, and others.

If you choose to use essential oils while on blood thinners, it is important that you are aware of the signs of bleeding so you can quickly identify when a potential drug-essential oil interaction occurs. If you experience nosebleeds, blood in the sink after brushing or flossing teeth, bruises that are larger than normal or do not heal in a timeframe that is normal for you, vomiting blood or a substance that looks like coffee grounds, blood in the stools or black-tarry stools, contact the person who monitors your anticoagulation.

#42

DO ESSENTIAL OILS INTERACT WITH BIRTH CONTROL PILLS?

YLANG YLANG
Cananga odorata

Short Answer

There is no human data to suggest that essential oils interact with birth control pills, however in vitro there is a theoretical risk at very high doses.

Birth control pills (more formally called oral contraceptives, OCs) are divided into two subgroups: there are combined oral contraceptives (containing both an estrogen and progesterone component, most common), and progesterone only pills (rarely prescribed). While essential oil constituents do not interact directly with the components of either, it is important to look at how the components are metabolized. For example, a progesterone-ish compound, drosperinone (found in Yasmin® and Yaz®) is metabolized by CYP3A4, and the estrogen component (ethinyl estradiol) is metabolized and oxidized by CYP3A4 and CYP2C9.

In vitro studies show that certain essential oil constituents can inhibit the function of CYP3A4 and 2C9. This is not surprising because CYP3A4 is notorious for having interactions with everything. Importantly, there are not essential oil constituents that induce either CYP3A4 or 2C9 (meaning that even theoretically, they cannot decrease levels of OCs, which would lead to an increased risk of unplanned pregnancy). Constituents and whole oils such as blue chamomile, peppermint, menthol, bergamottin, bergaptol, bergapten, psoralen and more have been shown to inhibit CYP3A4, and blue chamomile, α-bisabolol, chamazulene, farnesene has been shown to inhibit CPY2C9. If inhibition were to occur in humans, which it has not been shown to do, this would cause drug levels to increase, theoretically increasing the risk of side effects.

The only study I could find concluded that there was no evidence to suggest that orally-administered, encapsulated lavender oil interacts with oral contraceptive pills. Given the high doses required in animal and in vitro studies, there is likely no meaningful risk to women who are using oral contraceptives.

It's important to note that both essential oils and fatty oils can weaken latex condoms, so it is not suggested to use either with latex. Lambskin and polyurethane condoms can be used with fatty oils. Lambskin condoms are not vegetarian, and they are more porous than latex; therefore, they should only be used to prevent pregnancy as they cannot protect against every sexually transmitted infection.

While this is a book on essential oils, I feel I would be remiss if I did not mention that it is well known that the common herbal supplement St. John's Wort induces metabolism of OCs, thereby lowering drug levels and increasing the risk of unplanned pregnancy. If you choose to use St John's Wort while on OCs and do not wish to become pregnant, please use a back-up method (e.g. condom, spermicide, morning after pill). Tell your friends about this one; I am consistently impressed how many women use St. John's Wort while on OCs without knowledge of the interaction.

If you choose to use essential oils while on OCs, talk to your doctor and pharmacist about the side effects of your medicine, especially what to look out for to know if the levels are too high. Common side effects, especially upon initiation, include nausea, sore breasts, and headaches. More serious side effects include blood clots, hypertension, and increased risk of heart attack, and these risks are higher in women who smoke tobacco. Women on birth control, especially those over 35 years old, are urged not to smoke.

#43

CAN ESSENTIAL OILS CAUSE A FALSE POSITIVE ON A DRUG TEST?

SPEARMINT
Mentha spicata

Short Answer

Essential oils do not necessarily cause false positives
on drug tests; however, testing mechanisms
give false positive answers 5-10% of the time
and false negatives 10-15% of the time.

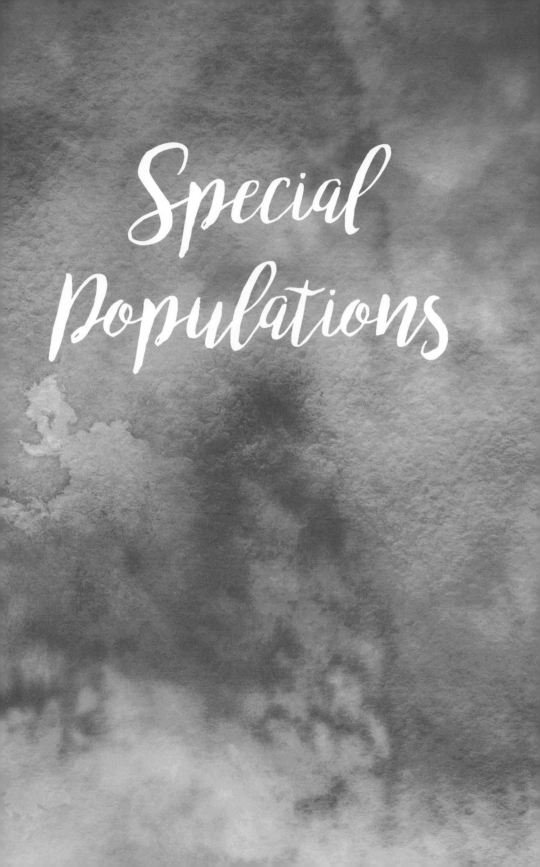

Special Populations

In this section, we will examine a few special populations such as children, women who are pregnant or nursing, and the elderly. As is usually the case with essential oils, the answer to the question of 'Can I use it?' remains 'It depends.' If you are considering using an essential oil for one of the above populations, be sure to keep in mind that it ultimately depends on previous experience with the essential oil, which oil you choose, and a myriad of other factors. Use your best judgment to guide you, never forget your carrier oil, and know that every body is different.

#44

WHAT ESSENTIAL OILS SHOULD I AVOID IF I AM PREGNANT OR NURSING?

FENNEL
Foeniculum vulgare

Short Answer

There is no definitive list of which oils should or should not be used when pregnant or nursing, but there is some data to consider if you want to be conservative.

Long Answer

There is no definitive list of which oils should or should not be used when pregnant or nursing (even though many different sources are happy to share their "Do Not Use Unless You Wish Imminent Doom" lists). Much of the fear surrounding the use of essential oils in pregnancy comes from lack of knowledge. I do not recommend for or against any essential oil during pregnancy and instead rely on the best judgment of the woman to decide what is appropriate for her. To answer this question fully, we will divide pregnancy into a variety of categories and look at fertility, implantation, placental crossing of essential oil constituents, embryotoxicity, fetotoxicity, teratogenicity, termination of pregnancy, childbirth, and breastfeeding.

Fertility is the first step toward pregnancy. For a woman to become pregnant, hormone levels of progesterone, estrogen, luteinizing hormone, follicle-stimulating hormone, and gonadotropin-releasing hormone all must work in concert to create an environment primed for pregnancy. In extraordinarily high doses, citral has impaired ovarian follicle function (commonly known as eggs); however, this was only after repeated injections in the belly (equivalent to 25 mL of lemongrass essential oil). Carrot seed essential oil (also at extremely high doses of 2.5-5 mL/kg injected subcutaneously, roughly equivalent to 175-350 mL in an average adult) blocked progesterone synthesis and implantation.

Several oils have been shown to have estrogenic activity, and estrogen spikes are necessary for ovulation. In vitro studies suggest that citral, geraniol, nerol, and (E)-anethole can displace estrogen from isolated receptors at high concentrations; however, they are not recognized by estrogen-responsive cell lines. It has been suggested that citral is estrogenic because it can bind the estrogen receptors, but it failed to produce any estrogenic activity in mice who had their ovaries removed. Another very old study demonstrated the estrogenic activity of anise, fennel, and (E)-anethole (a subsequent study said it is likely the polymers of anethole, not the individual molecule that is responsible). Bottom line, some essential oil constituents have been shown in vitro to have some estrogenic activity, but the activity is very weak. If you want to be conservative during this stage, you may consider limiting exposure to essential oils high in (E)-anethole such as anise, aniseed myrtle, star anise, and sweet and bitter fennel.

There is no data to suggest that essential oils pose a substantial risk to male fertility, nor is it likely that the estrogen activity described above is strong enough to interfere with oral contraceptive medicines (birth control pills).

Next, let's look at the implantation phase. Very high doses of subcutaneously-administered savin essential oil, and isolated (E)-anethole and bergapten given orally have been shown to reduce implantation of pups in mice and rats. However, if we extrapolate the data for bergapten to a human, it would require at approximately 1.5-3 kg of lime essential oil consumed by mouth; therefore, the data is not applicable to humans. (E)-anethole, even at very high doses, did not pose a threat to pups when given on days 1-2 of pregnancy, but pregnancy was prevented in all five animals when given on days 3-5, and in three of the five animals when given on day 6-10. You may choose to avoid excessive use of essential oils high in (E)-anethole listed above during the implantation phase.

Rapid cell differentiation is important for the newly developing embryo, and anything that blocks cell differentiation may lead to a failed pregnancy or a physical malformation. In a study

#45

ARE ESSENTIAL OILS SAFE TO USE FOR CHILDREN?

EUCALYPTUS
Eucalyptus radiata

Short Answer

Essential oils can be safely used for children. You can dilute essential oils in carrier oil, avoid application directly to the face or mucous membranes, and limit internal consumption of essential oils to increase the safety.

Long Answer

Essential oils for children remains a controversial topic with some recommending against use entirely in children less than 12 years old, and others recommending use like adult usage. My opinion is somewhere in the middle, and ultimately, I rely on the best judgment of parents to decide what is correct for their child. Just as stated in the section on pregnant women, I do not have one list of 'never use' essential oils for children.

When deciding how much oil to use on a child, some recommend dosage of essential oil based on body weight, and this seems reasonable to me. For a 30 kg (66 lb) child, the approximate dose would be 0.1-0.4 mL (3-12 drops)/24 hrs. Many parents choose to avoid direct ingestion of essential oils for children less than 20 kg (44 lb).

Skin does not fully develop until 3 months of age, and children have fewer metabolizing enzymes than their adult counterparts. Dilution is suggested for infants, even 1% (1 drop in 100 mL) may be warranted for very young infants. Some recommend against use at all in premature babies, and I agree that parents should exercise caution. Even with dilution, it may be wise to avoid oils that are very hot on the skin such as clove, cinnamon, oregano, or thyme when using with premature infants.

In the current report of the American Association of Poison Control Center, the number of poisonings due to essential oils between 2000-2014 increased, and this is often spun into headlines like "More Kids Accidentally Poisoned by Essential Oils." However, the data is not as alarming as the headlines suggest. There were 2,557,756 exposures to substances that were reported to a poison control center in 2014. Of those, 13,063 (0.51%) were related to essential oils, with

8,759 documented to have taken place in children less than 5 years old. Unidentified and miscellaneous oils were the most common, followed by tea tree oil, eucalyptus, cinnamon oil, and clove oil. The total number of reported serious incidents involving essential oils in 2014 was 203, which represents a mean increase of 10 per year since the last report. This is fewer than the increase and raw number reported serious incidents related to vitamins, cough and cold preparations, electrolytes and minerals, a whole slew of medications, and weapons of mass destruction. So, the risk of harm is not necessarily increasing, but the number of exposures is increasing and therefore the proportional reporting has increased.

Two oils particularly get a bad rap with children: peppermint oil and eucalyptus oil. While the essential oil name is commonly reported, it is the chemical constituents of menthol and 1,8-cineole contained within the essential oil that lead to the bad rap.

Peppermint oil is comprised of up to 55% menthol and up to 10% 1,8-cineole. In four children aged between 1 year and 3 years and 9 months, menthol and 1,8-cineole containing solutions have been shown to cause serious, non-fatal reactions when instilled nasally. The most serious reaction was when 1 mL of an unspecified menthol-containing solution was instilled into the nose of a child less than 2 years old who then lapsed into a coma. Others suffered mucous membrane irritation. Another child suffered from immediate collapse, rapid breathing, cyanosis, wheezing, and coughing. He recovered fully within a week.

Peppermint oil is not recommended by the National Association of Holistic Aromatherapy for children 30 months of age or less because the nasal mucosa is an autonomic reflexogen organ. The nose has a distant action to the heart, lungs and circulation and may lead to sudden apnea and glottal constriction. What is interesting about peppermint essential oil is that data suggests that it's not best to apply peppermint oil directly under the nose of infants and small children, but it has been extrapolated to suggestions like "avoid use in all children less than 12 years old." Also, one of the most commonly cited documents recommending against the use in children states specifically not to use menthol preparations directly under the nose, and makes no comment on other uses.

Menthol has been documented to cause neonatal jaundice in babies with a deficiency of glucose-6-phosphate dehydrogenase (G6PD) deficiency. Menthol is metabolized by a pathway that contains G6PD, so menthol may accumulate in people who are missing the enzyme. Given that menthol is a very common food ingredient, it is generally recognized as safe for human consumption by multiple national governments. So, the risk is not likely that high. However, it is recommended to avoid overuse in young children who are deficient in G6PD.

Both menthol and 1,8-cineole are TRPM8 agonists, which means that they produce a cold sensation. In animal models, both cold air and menthol slowed respiration due to stimulation of the cold receptor, and this has been replicated in premature infants. You may choose to avoid these essential oils in young children, especially if there is any underlying respiratory disorder.

Eucalyptus oil contains varying amounts of 1,8-cineole depending on the species of plant, with *Eucalyptus globulus* having up to 84%, *Eucalyptus radiata* up to 65% and *Eucalyptus polybractea* having up to 92%. The biggest concern with

1,8-cineole and eucalyptus oil is seizure. Seizures are a rare and unusual symptom of poisoning, even after ingestion of large amounts of oil. Based on all available data, some experts conclude that approximately 2% of children will experience a seizure after extensive exposure.

Let's move on and discuss individual reports. In a case review of 192 cases of accidental ingestion, four children suffered a seizure. Ingestion of 30 mL produced a fatal seizure in an 8-month old. Convulsions resulted when an 11-month old boy had 10-15 mL of eucalyptus spilled on his face and recovered without medical intervention. A 12-month old girl was given 5 prolonged baths in eucalyptus, thyme, and pine essential oil and had a seizure lasting about one minute, and a 4-year old with no history of seizures had a grand mal convulsion after exposure to a 11% eucalyptus solution compounded in an over the counter lice medication.

Is 1,8-cineole responsible for the convulsion activities (and therefore can using eucalyptus varieties lower in 1,8-cineole reduce the risk of seizure)? In animal models, isolated 1,8-cineole was shown to change calcium and potassium levels in the brain. Other studies demonstrate that 1,8-cineole is a central nervous system depressant, and some authors conclude that it would be too difficult for eucalyptus essential oil to produce such a strong activation required to induce a seizure. Most seizures that have been cited in the literature come from ingestion or extended inhalation of large quantities of eucalyptus oil; therefore, they may not represent a general seizure risk in all populations but just in large quantities in small children.

If you choose to use Eucalyptus oil for children, you may wish to use the *radiata* species as it has less 1,8-cineole than other species. If you can get your hands on some *Eucalyptus dives*, this is almost devoid of any 1,8-cineole.

Ultimately, it is up to parents to decide what is right for their child. If you are someone who decides not to use any oils on children, that is okay. If you are someone that decides to dilute, 1 drop in 10 drops of carrier oil or even 1 drop in 100 drops of carrier oil, that is okay. The choice is up to you; just remember the pharmacist's mantra: "start low and go slow."

#46

DOES LAVENDER OIL CAUSE BREAST SWELLING IN YOUNG BOYS?

GERANIUM
Pelargonium graveolens

Short Answer

Likely not; the case reports that conclude that lavender oil can cause breast swelling contain weak methodology and are very hotly contested.

Long Answer

The data regarding lavender oil and breast swelling in young boys is very hotly contested as evidenced by the number of response comments in *New England Journal of Medicine* and a response article entitled "Lack of Evidence that Essential Oils Affect Puberty."

The concern arises from one case series: there were three case reports published together said to link lavender and tea tree oil to gynecomastia. Three boys experienced gynecomastia despite normal serum hormone levels and being of normal health.

There were several very strong rebuttals to the methodology of this study. First, the authors didn't note the full list of ingredients in the products cited or account for estrogenic contaminants including plasticizers, pesticides, and herbicides. To confirm whether lavender affected hormones, they did laboratory tests, and obtained *Lavandula officinalis* from a chemical company as opposed to an essential oil company. To determine if the lavender oil was estrogenic and androgenic in cell culture, they diluted it in DSMO and cultured in polystyrene plates, both of which are said to modulate estrogens and androgens. Authors also chose to do a cell culture instead of a uterotropic assay (a test to determine if uterine lining grows in response to a chemical), and this has been widely criticized because uterotropic assays are considered the gold standard testing method. The authors themselves state that more research is needed to determine causality.

In my professional opinion, lavender oil and gynecomastia is a consideration, but would not preclude me from using in a young boy.

#47

CAN ESSENTIAL OILS I USE AFFECT MY CHILDREN?

HELICHRYSUM
Helichrysum italicum

Short Answer

If you use essential oils around your children, it is highly likely that they will be exposed to them as well. The method and duration of contact will determine if and how the child may be affected.

Long Answer

Before birth, maternal use of essential oils may lead to essential oil constituents passing from maternal blood through the placenta in the fetus's blood. After birth, family use of essential oils may be transferred to the baby via aromatic, topical, or oral exposure. Certainly, if an infant or child is in a room where essential oils are diffusing, they will be exposed to them.

Essential oils (as well as medications) are known to be excreted via the kidneys, lungs, skin, and feces. Therefore, if a child is exposed to urine, feces, or your breath after you have used an essential oil (or eaten constituents of essential oils in foods), he or she may be exposed to constituents of essential oils. Even if you have not applied an essential oil to the skin recently, you may have excreted essential oil constituents on your skin, and a child may be exposed while being held.

Most substances pass from maternal plasma to breastmilk, and essential oils are likely to be excreted in the breast milk. The important thing is to remember is that the exposure is minimal, and exposure to essential oils does not necessarily confer any risk to the child. To prevent any excessive exposure, you may consider a few cautions. If you recently put undiluted essential oils on your chest or breast, you may choose to avoid holding the infants and very young children skin-to-skin until the essential oil has absorbed into the skin. You also may choose to avoid breastfeeding for a period – perhaps 30 minutes to 1 hour.

Consider diffusing around infants only in well-ventilated rooms and for short periods of time until the child becomes accustomed to essential oils.

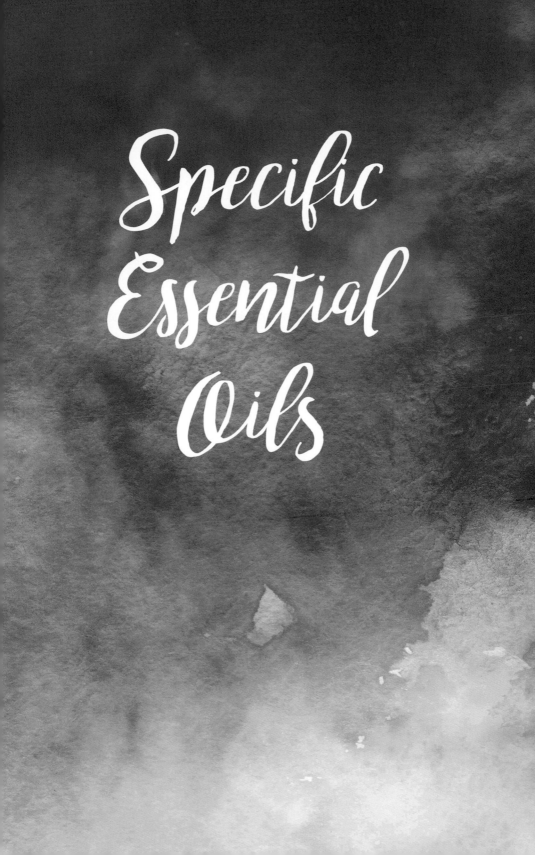

Specific
Essential
Oils

Occasionally, there are concerns about a specific essential oil or a specific essential oil constituent, and other times there are multiple essential oils from similar plant genre, and it is necessary to compare. In this section, we will discuss concerns specifically about tea tree oil, and compare varieties of lavender and frankincense.

#48

I'VE READ THAT TEA TREE ESSENTIAL OIL IS EXTREMELY DANGEROUS. WHAT ARE THE REAL RISKS?

TEA TREE
Melaleuca alternifolia

Short Answer

As with all essential oils, tea tree oil can be dangerous in very large doses. Tea tree oil is also more prone to oxidation than other essential oils, and when oxidized, it is more likely to cause skin irritation.

Long Answer

Tea tree essential oil is an excellent addition to skin and hair care products, and is highly valued for toning skin. It may also be used in a bath to invigorate the skin.

Tea tree essential oil may cause skin irritation in some people. In a non-systematic case review, skin reactions such as contact dermatitis, eczema, hypersensitivity, redness, and blistering have occurred, with the most common reaction being contact dermatitis; most episodes subsided after discontinuation of the product. It was stated in a personal communication in spring 2015 that a large, international essential oil company has received one report of mild, transient skin irritation following application of tea tree essential oil according to label instructions. This represents less than 0.005% of all people who purchased tea tree essential oil in the US during that time.

When exposed to excessive heat, light, or air, tea tree oil can oxidize more quickly than other essential oils. The oxidation leads to changes in the chemical structures in the essential oil, and the newly formed compounds are more irritating to the skin; therefore, there may be an added risk of irritation from tea tree oil that has been improperly stored.

Tea tree essential oil is not labeled for oral use, and ingestion of <10 mL in children and 30 mL in an adult has been reported to cause adverse effects. Ingestion of a much larger amount in a 60-year-old man ('1/2 cup' or ~120 mL) led to a semiconscious state, hallucinations with subsequent diarrhea, and abdominal pain for six weeks. Ingestion of tea tree oil is not generally recommended, and ingestion of many milliliters of essential oil is not recommended for any essential oil.

When stored properly, tea tree essential oil is unlikely to oxidize, and the risk of skin reaction is low. Toxicity after ingesting very large amounts of tea tree oil has occurred, and ingestion of large quantities of any essential oil are not recommended. However, the labeling of tea tree as a 'very dangerous' essential oil on select blogs and online writings is an exaggeration in my opinion.

#49

WHAT ARE THE DIFFERENCES IN FRANKINCENSE SPECIES?

FRANKINCENSE
Boswellia sacra

Short Answer

While all the frankincense species are from the same family of plants, the different varieties contain different levels of terpene constituents, and there is much variability in the levels of incensole diterpenes.

Long Answer

Probably one of the most famous essential oils out there, frankincense is almost legendary. There are several varieties of Frankincense: *Boswellia carterii*, *Boswellia sacra*, and *Boswellia frereana*. These plants are resin tapped, and the essential oil is steam distilled from the resin. All three are from the Burseracea line of plants, but *carterii* is found in Somalia and Yemen, *sacra* is found in Oman, and *frereana* in Somalia. Some authors contend that *sacra* and *carterii* are the same species of plant, but from different regions. Whether they are the same species or different, I don't know; however, the chemical natures of these are different:

1. *Carterii* is primarily comprised of alpha-pinene with lower amounts of limonene, myrcene, alpha-thujene and good levels of the diterpenes incensole.
2. *Sacra* is overwhelmingly alpha-pinene, and high levels of diterpenes incensole.
3. *Frerana* is primarily alpha-thujene, alpha-pinene, para-cymene.

Though *carterii* and *frereana* are harvested and distilled similarly, the chemical natures could not be more different. *Frereana* is completely devoid of diterpene boswelic acids in the incensole family, whereas *sacra* has higher levels than *carterii*.

So, who cares about incensoles anyways? Well, research has looked at how incensole acetate interacts with the body and found that it activates certain receptors called the TRPV-3 receptors. This can make *carterii* feel warm on the skin and interact with different brain channels, which produce feelings of calm and spiritual exaltation. Some people claim that the lack of incensole acetate makes *frereana* an inferior version of frankincense, but I disagree. I think that it simply makes it different than the other frankincenses. In some cultures, *frereana* is considered the King of all Frankincense.

The aromas of the oils are distinct. *Carterii* and *sacra* have rich, woodsy aromas perfect for spiritual practices whereas *frereana* has a lemony-bright aroma makes it perfect for diffusion. All three are great for the skin, and frankincense supports normal cellular function when taken internally.

So, how do you pick between them? *Carterii* is a bit less expensive than *sacra* and is more familiar, accessible, and understandable to most people. If you want a brighter aroma, consider the *frereana*.

If you don't know where to start, any frankincense can be added to skin care routines or spiritual practice.

Example uses of frankincense:
- Add a drop of frankincense *carterii* to a toothbrush before brushing.
- Diffuse *frereana* with cedarwood and vetiver.
- Create a body butter with orange and *carterii*.
- Meditate or do yoga with *sacra* on the crown of your head.

#50

WHAT IS THE DIFFERENCE BETWEEN SPECIES OF LAVENDER?

LAVANDIN
Lavandula x intermedia

Short Answer

There are two primary varieties of lavender:
the true lavenders and lavandins, and each
of these has many subspecies.

Long Answer

There are two primary different varieties of lavender, both of which have subvarieties: *Lavandula angustifolia* (aka *Lavandula officialis*, aka lavender, aka English lavender) and *Lavandula x intermedia*, commonly called lanvadin. *L. angustifolia* is the true lavender species, whereas *Lavandula x intermedia* is a hybrid between *L. angustifolia* and *L. latifolia* (spike lavender). Lavandin plants are typically larger with more pointed, spiked flowers. The flowers are usually more lateral and emerge later than *L. angustifolia* flowers. Lavender comes in varieties such as Royal Velvet, Hidcote, Vera, and Munstead. Lavandin comes in many varieties including Provence, Giant Hidcote, Grosso, and Phenomenal.

The hybridization of the plant does not necessarily negate it as a source for essential oil; in fact lavandin is the common version of lavender used in perfumery because it is less expensive, and the chemical profile of the distilled oil is more consistently the same. The yield and chemical composition of the essential oils are slightly different between the two types of plant. Lavandin plants typically produce more essential oil per plant than lavender (partially attributed to its large size). The essential oil obtained from *L. angustifolia* flowers is composed primarily of linalyl acetate, linalool, lavandulol, 1,8-cineol, lavandulyl acetate and camphor, while the essential oil from *L. x intermedia* contains linalool, linalyl acetate, camphor, 1,8-cineol and borneol. Lavandin contains more camphor (around 7%), which gives it a slightly more medicinal and less floral smell.

Spike lavender varieties such as *Lavandula stoechas* and *Lavendula latifolia* (aka Spanish lavender) produce even more camphorated oil, and because of this, the distillates are not used in aromatherapy but in more industrial uses such as in paints.

FIGURE 1: *Lavandula angustifolia*

FIGURE 2: *Lavandula x intermedia*

More
Essentials

#1

DO DIGESTIVE ENZYMES INTERACT WITH MEDICINES?

Short Answer

There are some theoretical interactions between digestive enzymes and medications and supplements.

Long Answer

There are a variety of medications and supplements that include cellulose as an excipient, which helps to ensure that there is delayed release technology inside tablets and capsules. If you take a digestive enzyme that contains cellulase (the enzyme that breaks down cellulose), you may theoretically affect the medication's delayed release technology.

The therapeutic action of medications that act in the gut to prevent absorption of carbohydrates such as acarbose and miglitol may be altered by the addition of enzymes that break down carbohydrates including amylase.

The digestive enzymes bromelain and papain may interact with blood-thinning medicines such as warfarin, aspirin, dabigatran, rivaroxaban, and apixiban.

If you choose to use digestive enzymes while taking a medication, be sure to identify if the medicine contains cellulose, check your blood sugar frequently if you are on acarbose or miglitol, and know the signs and symptoms of bleeding and clotting if you are taking a blood thinner.

#2

WHY IS THERE SO MUCH MAGNESIUM IN CERTAIN CALCIUM SUPPLEMENTS?

Short Answer

Magnesium and calcium are intimately connected and have opposing actions in the body, therefore it is recommended to include magnesium alongside calcium supplementation to ensure that calcium does not become over-abundant in the body (which can lead to various deleterious effects).

Long Answer

Calcium is an important part of bone health, but it is not the only key player. Unopposed calcium can be very dangerous to the heart; therefore, it is key to balance calcium with magnesium. Magnesium does three key things that promote bone and heart health. First, magnesium increases the level of calcitonin, and this "tones down calcium" levels in the blood, and this drives calcium into the bones. Calcium levels in the blood are decreased by increased deposition of calcium ions in the bones and thereby decreases deposition in soft tissues. Magnesium is a cofactor for alkaline phosphatase, and this is an enzyme that aids in the formation of calcium crystals in the bones.

In the cardiovascular system, calcium and magnesium play opposing roles whereby calcium constricts musculature and causes vasoconstriction and magnesium causes relaxation of blood vessels and musculature. Magnesium is such an effective relaxant in the cardiovascular system that it is the drug of choice to treat urgent cases of high blood pressure in pregnancy, and supplementation of magnesium has been shown in multiple studies to be an effective treatment for high blood pressure in people who are not pregnant as well.

Some estimates conclude that up to 70% of the population of the United States is magnesium deficient, whereas magnesium deficiencies are rare in undeveloped nations. This may be because processed foods and meats are relatively devoid of magnesium, but magnesium is abundant in beans and legumes. Importantly, these are usually subclinical deficiencies, with no overt symptoms and no abnormalities on blood analysis.

Therefore, magnesium is commonly added to calcium supplements to ensure that calcium can be optimally effective and prevent the adverse effects of unopposed calcium.

#3

CAN I TAKE MSM IF I AM ALLERGIC TO SULFA MEDICATIONS?

Short Answer

Yes.

Long Answer

The most well-known medications that cause sulfa allergies include certain antibiotics, anti-HIV medications, anti-diabetic medications, diuretics, and many others. The symptoms of sulfa reactions range from a mild rash to a serious, life-threatening skin conditions.

Methylsulfonylmethane is a small organosulfur compound that naturally occurs in cow's milk, coffee, tomatoes, Swiss chard, corn, and alfalfa. People with sulfa drug allergies may safely take MSM-containing products, and here is why.

Sulfonamide bonds are the reason that certain medications cause sulfa allergies, and MSM does not contain a sulfonamide bond. In the chemical structures below, you can see the sulfur atom (the "S") sitting right next to the nitrogen atom (the "N"). This is known as a sulfonamide bond, and can be allergenic in humans and animals. To contrast, the MSM molecule does not contain nitrogen or a sulfonamide bond, and therefore does not carry the same risk as an allergen.

Evidence suggests that MSM is non-toxic, and that supplementation of approximately 3 g/day for 30 days reveals no side effects. Much higher doses (1.5 g/kg/day) have been given to animals for a longer period of time, and there have no side effects or increases in mortality. My research revealed no reported cases of allergies to MSM.

In my professional opinion, MSM is safe for people with sulfa allergies, and studies have shown very little risk of side effects. If a rash or any other symptoms of allergy occurs, stop the use of MSM and consult a health care professional.

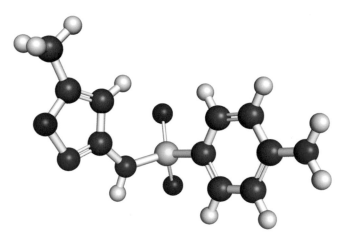

FIGURE 1: Structure of Sulfonamide

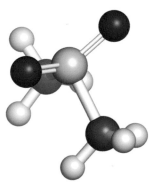

FIGURE 2: Structure of Methylsulfonylmethane

GLOSSARY

1. **ALDEHYDE:** an organic compound containing the group – CHO, formed by the oxidation of alcohols. Typical aldehydes include methanol (formaldehyde) and ethanol (acetaldehyde).

2. **CROSS-ALLERGENICITY:** Cross-reactivity applies to the reaction between two different species as opposed to the self-reactivity. For example, this a cross-allergenicity could arise if you are allergic to both a rosemary plant and sensitive to a rosemary essential oil.

3. **CROSS-REACTIVITY:** Cross-reactivity applies to the reaction between two different species. This is similar to cross-allergenicity.

4. **DITERPENE:** any of a group of terpenes found in plant gums and resins, having unsaturated molecules based on a unit with the formula $C_{20}H_{32}$.

5. **ETHER:** a pleasant-smelling and colorless volatile liquid that is highly flammable. It is used as an anaesthetic and as a solvent or intermediate in industrial processes.

6. **ESTER:** an organic compound made by replacing the hydrogen of an acid by an alkyl or other organic group. Many naturally occurring fats and essential oils are esters of fatty acids.

7. **EXCIPIENT:** an inactive substance that serves as the vehicle or medium for a drug or other active substance.

8. **FURANOCOUMARIN:** A class of organic chemical compounds produced by a variety of plants. The chemical structure of furanocoumarins consists of a furan ring fused with coumarin.

9. **G6PD:** Glucose-6-phosphate dehydrogenase deficiency (G6PD deficiency), also known as favism (after the fava bean), is an X-linked recessive inborn error of metabolism that predisposes to hemolysis (spontaneous destruction of red blood cells) and resultant jaundice in response to a number of triggers, such as certain foods, illness, or medication.

10. **HYDROLYSIS:** The reaction of water with another chemical compound to form two or more products, involving ionization of the water molecule and usually splitting the other compound. Examples include the catalytic conversion of starch to glucose, saponification, and the formation of acids or bases from dissolved ions.

11. **IN VITRO:** (of a process) performed or taking place in a test tube, culture dish, or elsewhere outside a living organism.

12. **IN VIVO:** (of processes) performed or taking place in a living organism.

13. **ISOPRENE:** a volatile liquid hydrocarbon, whose molecule forms the basic structural unit of essential oils and rubber.

14. **KETONE:** an organic compound containing a carbonyl group =C=O bonded to two hydrocarbon groups, made by oxidizing secondary alcohols. The simplest such compound is acetone.

15. **LACTONE:** an organic compound containing an ester group – OCO – as part of a ring.

16. **MONOTERPENE:** Monoterpenes are a class of terpenes that consist of two isoprene units and have the molecular formula C10H16.

17. **OXIDATION:** the process or result of oxidizing or being oxidized. To combine with oxygen; make into an oxide or to increase the positive charge or valence of (an element) by removing electrons.

18. **PHARMACOKINETICS:** a branch of pharmacology concerned with the movement of drugs in the body.

19. **PHENOL:** any compound with a hydroxyl group linked directly to a benzene ring.

20. **PHYTOALEXINS:** a substance that is produced by plant tissues in response to contact with a parasite and specifically inhibits the growth of that parasite.

21. **REDUCTION:** To decrease the valence of (an atom) by adding electrons. To remove oxygen from (a compound). To add hydrogen to (a compound). To change to a metallic state by removing nonmetallic constituents; smelt.

22. **SESQUITERPENE:** a terpene with the formula C15H24, or a simple derivative of such a compound.

23. **SUBSTRATE:** the substance on which an enzyme acts.

REFERENCES

QUESTION 1

1. Shawe, K. (1996). The Biological Role of Essential Oils, Aromatherapy Quarterly, 50, 23-27.
2. Cseke L, Kaufman PB, Kirakosyan A. The biology of essential oils in the pollination of flowers. Natural Product Communications 2007;2(12):1317-1336
3. Kitic D, Pavlovic D, Brankovic S. The role of essential oils and the biological detoxification in the prevention of aflatoxin borne diseases. Curr Top Med Chem. 2013;13(21):2767-90.
4. Peighami-Ashnaei S, Farzaneh M, Sharifi-Tehrani A, Behboudi K. Effect of essential oils in control of plant diseases. Commun Agric Appl Biol Sci. 2009;74(3):843-7.
5. Arshad Z, Hanif MF, Qadri RWK, Khan MM. Role of Essential Oils in Plant Diseases Protection: A Review. International Journal of Chemical and Biochemical Science 2014; 6: 11-17

QUESTION 2

1. Are essential oils safe? How to complete a patch test. Available at: https://www.takingcharge.csh.umn.edu/explore-healing-practices/aromatherapy/are-essential-oils-safe. Last accessed March 11, 2017.
2. Tisserand, R and Rodney Young. Essential Oil Safety: A Guide for Health Care Professionals. 2nd ed. 2013. Churchill-Livingstone.

QUESTION 3

1. Code of Federal Regulations Title 21. Food and Drugs. Substances Generally Recognized as Safe. Available at: https://www.accessdata.fda.gov/scripts/cdrh/cfdocs/cfcfr/CFRSearch.cfm?fr=182.20. Last Accessed March 2, 2017.
2. McCormick MA and Manoguerra AS. Toxicity of Pennyroyal Oil: A Case report and review. Vet Hum Toxicol. 1988, 30, 347
3. Sullivan JB, Rumack BH, Thomas H et al. Pennyroyal oil poisoning and hepatotoxicity. J Am Med Assoc 1979; 242:2768-75
4. Choi J, Lee KT, Ka H et al. Constituents of the essential oil of the Cinnamomum cassia stem bark and the biological properties. Arch of Pharmaceutic Res. 2001; 24;418-23.
5. Hartnoll G, Moore D, Douek D. Near fatal ingestion of oil of cloves. Arch Dis Child. 1993; 69;392-2

6. Janes SE, Price CS, Thomas D. Essential oil poisoning: N-acetylcysteine for eugenol-induced heaptic failure and analysis of a national database. Eu J Pediatr. 2005: 164, 520-2
7. Thorup I, Würtzen G, Castensen J et al. Short term toxicity study in rats dosed with pulegone and menthol. Toxicol Lett 1983b; 19:207-10

QUESTION 4

1. Chadwick M, Trewin H, Gawthrop F, and Wagstaff C. Sesquiterpenoids Lactones: Benefits to Plants and People. Int J Mol Sci. 2013 Jun 19;14(6):12780-805. Available at: https://www.ncbi.nlm.nih.gov/pmc/articles/PMC3709812/ Last accessed 12/26/2016.
2. Bhattacharya, A et al. Review: The roles of plant phenolics in defence and communication during Agrobacterium and Rhizobium infection. Mol Plant Pathol. 2010. 11 (5): 705–19. doi:10.1111/j.1364-3703.2010.00625.x. Available at: http://onlinelibrary.wiley.com/doi/10.1111/j.1364-3703.2010.00625.x/abstract;jsessionid=0750DAB7EC988EFCDEC08A5B9FB6F47B.f03t03 Last accessed 12/26/2016.
3. Plant Resins: Chemistry, evolution, ecology, and ethnobotany, by Jean Langenheim, Timber Press, Portland, Oregon. 2003
4. Steinberg, P. D. (1984). "Algal Chemical Defense Against Herbivores: Allocation of Phenolic Compounds in the Kelp Alaria marginata". Science. 223 (4634): 405–407. doi:10.1126/science.223.4634.405. PMID 17829890.
5. Powley MW, Carlson GP. Cytochrome P450 isozymes involved in the metabolism of phenol, a benzene metabolite. Toxicol Lett. 2001 Dec 1

QUESTION 5

1. How are essential oils extracted? National Association for Holistic Aromatherapy. Available at: https://naha.org/explore-aromatherapy/about-aromatherapy/how-are-essential-oils-extracted/. Last accessed March 1, 2017.

QUESTION 6

1. Ziegler M, Brandauer H, Ziegler E et al. A different aging model for orange oil: deterioration products. J Essential Oil Res. 1991 (3), 209-220.
2. Kalhberg AT, Shao LP, Nillson U. Hydroperoxides in oxidized d-limonene. Arch Dermatol Res. 1994 (26) 332-340

3   Karlberg AT, Magnusson K, Nilsson K, et al. Influence of an antioxidant on the formation of allergenic compounds during auto-oxidation of d-limonene. Ann Occup Hyg. 1994 (38) 199-207.

4. Gopalakrishnan N. Studies on the storage quality of CO2 extracted cardamom and clove bud oils. J Agric Food Chem. 1994 (42) 796-798.

5. Tisserand, R and Rodney Young. Essential Oil Safety: A Guide for Health Care Professionals. 2nd ed. 2013. Churchill-Livingstone.

QUESTION 7

1. Chamorro ER, Zambón SN, Morales WG, Sequeira AF and Velasco GA. Study of the Chemical Composition of Essential Oils by Gas Chromatography. Gas Chromatography in Plant Science, Wine Technology, Toxicology and Some Specific Applications. Available at: http://www.frre.utn.edu.ar/quimobi/clean/files/get/item/1870. Last Accessed March 11, 2017.

2. Tisserand, R and Rodney Young. Essential Oil Safety: A Guide for Health Care Professionals. 2nd ed. 2013. Churchill-Livingstone.

3. De Falco E, Mancini E, Roscigno G, Mignola E et al. Chemical Composition and Biological Activity of Essential Oils of *Origanum vulgare* L. subsp. *vulgare* L. under Different Growth Conditions. Molecules 2013, 18, 14948-14960; doi:10.3390/molecules181214948.

4. Viuda-Martos M, Ruíz-Navajas Y, Fernández-López J, Pérez-Álvarez JA. Chemical Composition of the Essential Oils Obtained From Some Spices Widely Used in Mediterranean Region. Acta Chim. Slov. 2007, 54, 921–926.

5. McCormick, D. B. 2006. Vitamins, Structure and Function of. Reviews in Cell Biology and Molecular Medicine.

QUESTION 8

1. American Academy of Allergy, Asthma, and Immunology. Allergy. Available at: https://www.aaaai.org/conditions-and-treatments/conditions-dictionary/allergy. Last accessed February 7, 2017.

2. Australasian Society of Clinical Immunology and Allergy. What is Allergy? Available at: https://www.allergy.org.au/patients/about-allergy/what-is-allergy

3. Hapten. Available at: https://www.britannica.com/science/hapten. Last Accessed: February 9, 2017.

4. Hypersensitivity: Immune Complex Mediated (Type III). Available at: http://www.els.net/WileyCDA/ElsArticle/refId-a0001138.html. Last accessed February 9, 2017.

5. Antibody-mediated (type II) hypersensitivity. Available at: http://missinglink.ucsf.edu/lm/immunology_module/prologue/objectives/obj11.html. Last Accessed February 7, 2017.
6. Diba VC and Statham BN. Contact urticaria from cinnamal leading to anaphylaxis. Contact Dermatitis. 2003. 46:119.
7. Lessenger JE. Occupational acute anaphylactic reaction to assault by perfume spray in the face. J Am Board Fam Pract. 2001. 14:137-140.
8. Starke JC. Photoallergy to sandalwood oil. Arch Dermatol. 1967. 96:62-63.
9. Goririz R, Delgado-Jimenez Y, Sanchez-Perez J. Photoallergic contact dermatitis from lavender oil in topical ketoprofen. Contact Dermatitis. 2007. 57:381-382
10. Zaynoun et al. A study of bergamot and its importance as a phototoxic agent. II. Factors which affect the phototoxic reaction induced by bergamot oil and psoralen derivatives. Contact Dermatitis 1977. 3:225-239.
11. Zaynoun et al. Johnson BE. A study of oil of bergamot and it importance as a phototoxic agent. I. Characterisation and quantification of the photoactive component. Br J Dermatol. 1977b. 96, 475-482.
12. Pirker C, Hausen BM, Uter W et al. Sensitization to tea tree oil in Germany and Austria. A multicenter study of the German Contact Dermatitis Group. J Dtsch Dermatol Ges. 2003. 2: 629-634
13. Frosch PJ, Pilz B, Andersen KE et al. Patch testing with fragrances: results of a multicenter study of the European Environmental & Contact Dermatitis Research Group with 48 frequently used constituents on perfumes. Contact Dermatitis. 1995. 33: 333-342.
14. Kaidbey KH and Kligman AM. Identification of contact photosensitizers by human assay. Current Concepts in Cutaneous Toxicity. Academic Press, New York.
15. Scheinman PL. Allergic contact dermatitis to fragrance: a review. Am J Contact Dermat. 1996. 7, 65-66.
16. Tisserand, R and Rodney Young. Essential Oil Safety: A Guide for Health Care Professionals. 2nd ed. 2013. Churchill-Livingstone.

QUESTION 9

1. Google. Available at: www.google.com. Last accessed February 15, 2017.
2. PubMed. Available at: https://www.ncbi.nlm.nih.gov/pubmed/. Last Accessed February 9, 2017
3. Natural Medicines Database. Available at: https://naturalmedicines.therapeuticresearch.com/. Last Accessed February 9, 2017

4. Pitchford, Paul. *Healing with Whole Foods: Oriental Traditions and Modern Nutrition* Berkeley, Calif: North Atlantic Books, 1996. Print.

5. Purves D, Augustine GJ, Fitzpatrick D, Katz LC, LaMantia AS, McNamara JO, Williams SM. Neuroscience, 2nd edition. Sunderland (MA): Sinauer Associates; 2001.

6. Johnson MH. Essential Reproduction, 7th Ed. February 2013, ©2012, Wiley-Blackwell

7. Hillery A, Lloyd AW, Swarbick J. Drug Delivery and Targeting: For Pharmacists and Pharmaceutical Scientists. Available at: http://ajprd.com/downloadebooks_pdf/37.pdf. Last accessed February 15, 2017.

8. Stewart D. The Chemistry of Essential Oils Made Simple. Care Publications, 2005

9. Young G, Lawrence R, Schreuder M. Ningxia Wolfberry: The Ultimate Superfood

10. Essential Oils Desk Reference. Life Science Publishing. 2015.

11. Schnaubelt K. The Healing Intelligence of Essential Oils: The Science of Advanced Aromatherapy. Inner Traditions / Bear & Co, 8 Nov 2011

12. Buckle J. Clinical Aromatherapy: Essential Oils in Practice. 2nd ed. Churchill Livingstone. 2003.

QUESTION 10

1. Transportation Security Administration. Liquids Rule. Available at: https://www.tsa.gov/travel/security-screening/liquids-rule. Last accessed February 15, 2017.

2. Handschuh H, O'Dwyer J, Adley CC. Bacteria that Travel: The Quality of Aircraft Water. Int J Environ Res Public Health. 2015 Nov; 12(11): 13938–13955. Available at: https://www.ncbi.nlm.nih.gov/pmc/articles/PMC4661625/ . Last Accessed February 15, 2017.

3. Handschuh H, Ryan MP, O'Dwyer J, Adley CC. Assessment of the Bacterial Diversity of Aircraft Water: Identification of the Frequent Fliers. PLoS ONE 12(1):e0170567. doi:10.1371/journal.pone.0170567. Available at: http://journals.plos.org/plosone/article/file?id=10.1371/journal.pone.0170567&type=printable. Last accessed February 15, 2017.

QUESTION 11

1. Purves D, Augustine GJ, Fitzpatrick D, Katz LC, LaMantia AS, McNamara JO, and Williams SM (eds). Neuroscience, 3rd edition. Sunderland (MA): Sinauer Associates; 2001.

QUESTION 12

1. Baeten KM and Akassoglou K. Extracellular Matrix and Matrix Receptors in Blood-Brain Barrier Formation and Stroke. Dev Neurobiol. 2011 Nov; 71(11): 1018–1039.
2. Purves D, Augustine GJ, Fitzpatrick D, Katz LC, LaMantia AS, McNamara JO, and Williams SM (eds). Neuroscience, 3rd edition. Sunderland (MA): Sinauer Associates; 2001.
3. Tao-Cheng JH, Nagy Z, Brightman MW. Tight junctions of brain endothelium in vitro are enhanced by astroglia. J Neurosci. 1987 Oct; 7(10):3293-9
4. Banks W. Characteristics of compounds that cross the blood-brain barrier. BMC Neurol. 2009; 9(Suppl 1): S3.
5. Kimelberg HK, Jalonen T, Walz W. (1993). Regulation of the brain microenvironment:transmitters and ions.In Murphy, S. Astrocytes: pharmacology and function. San Diego, CA: Academic Press. pp. 193–222.
6. Swaminathan N (1 October 2008). Brain-scan mystery solved. Scientific American Mind: 7.
7. Figley CR and Stroman PW (2011). "The role(s) of astrocytes and astrocyte activity in neurometabolism, neurovascular coupling, and the production of functional neuroimaging signals". European Journal of Neuroscience 33 (4): 577–588.

QUESTION 13

1. Poolman B., Driessen A.J.M., Konings W.N. Regulation of solute transport in Streptococci by external and internal pH values. Microbiol. Rev. 1987;51:498–508.
2. Trumpower B.L., Gennis R.B. Energy transduction by cytochrome complexes in mitochondrial and bacterial respiration: the enzymology of coupling electron transfer reactions to transmembrane proton translocation. Ann. Rev. Biochem. 1994;63:675–716. doi: 10.1146/annurev.bi.63.070194.003331.
3. Andrews R.E., Parks L.W., Spence K.D. Some effects of Douglas fir terpenes on certain microorganisms. Appl. Environ. Microbiol. 1980;40:301–304.
4. Uribe S., Ramirez T., Pena A. Effects of β-pinene on yeast membrane functions. J. Bacteriol. 1985;161:1195–1200.
5. Knobloch K., Pauli A., Iberl B. Antibacterial activity and antifungal properties of essential oil components. J. Essent. Oils Res. 1988;1:119–128. doi: 10.1080/10412905.1989.9697767.
6. Gill A.O., Holley R.A. Disruption of *E. coli*, *Listeria monocytogenes* and *Lactobacillus sakei* cellular membranes by plant oil aromatics. Int. J. Food Microbiol. 2006;108:1–9. doi: 10.1016/j.ijfoodmicro.2005.10.009.

7   Helander I.M., Alakomi H.L., Latva K., Mattila-Sandholm T., Pol I., Smid E.J., Gorris L.G.M., von Wright A. Characterization of the action of selected essential oil components on Gram-negative bacteria. J. Agric. Food Chem. 1998;46:3590–3595.

8. Ultee A., Bennik M.H., Moezelaar R. The phenolic hydroxyl group of carvacrol is essential for action against the food-borne pathogen *Bacillus cereus*. Appl. Environ. Microbiol. 2002;68:1561–1568. doi: 10.1128/AEM.68.4.1561-1568.2002.

9. Ultee A, Kets EP, Alberda M, Hoekstra FA, Smid EJ. Adaptation of the food-borne pathogen Bacillus cereus to carvacrol. Arch Microbiol. 2000 Oct; 174(4):233-8.

10. Bell HC, Wyllie SG, Warmington JR. Effects of tea tree oil on Escherichia coli. Lett Appl Microbiol. 1998 Mar; 26(3):194-8.

11. Lambert RJ, Skandamis PN, Coote PJ, Nychas GJ. A study of the minimum inhibitory concentration and mode of action of oregano essential oil, thymol and carvacrol. J Appl Microbiol. 2001 Sep; 91(3):453-62.

12. Juven BJ, Kanner J, Schved F, Weisslowicz H. J Appl Bacteriol. Factors that interact with the antibacterial action of thyme essential oil and its active constituents. 1994 Jun; 76(6):626-31.

13. Burt S. Essential oils: their antibacterial properties and potential applications in foods--a review. Int J Food Microbiol. 2004 Aug 1; 94(3):223-53.

14. Tassou C., Koutsoumanis K., Nychas J.E. Inhibition of *Salmonella enteritidis* and *Staphylococcus aureus* in nutrient broth by mint essential oil. Food Res. Int. 2000;33:273–280. doi: 10.1016/ S0963-9969(00)00047-8.

15. De Martino L, De Feo V, Fratianni F, Nazzaro F. Chemistry, antioxidant, antibacterial and antifungal activities of volatile oils and their components. Nat Prod Commun. 2009 Dec; 4(12):1741-50.

16. De Martino L, De Feo V, Nazzaro F Chemical composition and in vitro antimicrobial and mutagenic activities of seven Lamiaceae essential oils. Molecules. 2009 Oct 20; 14(10):4213-30.

QUESTION 14

1. Code of Federal Regulations Title 21. Food and Drugs. Substances Generally Recognized as Safe. Available at: https:// www.accessdata.fda.gov/scripts/cdrh/cfdocs/cfcfr/CFRSearch. cfm?fr=182.20. Last Accessed March 11, 2017.

QUESTION 15

1. Wester RC, Maibach HI. Regional variation in percutaneous absorption. In: Bronaugh RL, Maibach HI (eds). Percutaneous Absorption: Drugs, Cosmetics, Mechanisms, Methodology. New York: Marcel Dekker,1999:107–16.
2. Barker N, Hadgraft J, Rutter N. Skin permeability in the newborn. J Invest Dermatol. 1987 Apr;88(4):409-11.
3. Harpin VA, Rutter N. Barrier properties of the newborn infant's skin. J Pediatr. 1983 Mar;102(3):419-25.
4. Christophers E, Kligman AM. Percutaneous absorption in aged skin. In: Montagna W, ed. Advances in biology of the skin. Vol 6: Aging. Long Island City: Pergaman Press, 1965; p163–75.
5. DeSalva SJ, Thompson G. Na22Cl skin clearance in humans and its relation to skin age. J Invest Dermatol. 1965 Nov;45(5):315–8.
6. Tagami H. Functional characteristics of aged skin. Acta Dermatol Kyoto (English Edition). 1972;67:131–8.
7. Roskos KV, Maibach HI, Guy RH. The effect of aging on percutaneous absorption in man. J Pharmacokinet Biopharm 1989;17(6): 623
8. Williams, C. M. Using medications appropriately in older adults. *Am Fam Physician*, 2002;66(10), 1917.
9. Beers, M. H. Aging as a risk factor for medication-related problems. 1999. Available at: http://courses.washington.edu/pharm492/Week2/aging.pdf. Last accessed February 6, 2017.
10. Denda M, Koyama J, Hori J, Horii I, Takahashi M, Hara M, Tagami H. Age- and sex-dependent change in stratum corneum sphingolipids. Arch Dermatol Res, 285 (1993), pp. 415–417
11. Miller RA. The aging immune system: primer and prospectus. Science, 273 (1996), pp. 70–74
12. Sauder DN. Effect of age on epidermal immune function. Dermatol Clin, 4 (1986), pp. 447–454

QUESTION 19

1. Khalilzadeh E, Hazrati R, Saiah GV. Effects of topical and systemic administration of Eugenia caryophyllata buds essential oil on corneal anesthesia and analgesia. Res Pharm Sci. 2016 Jul;11(4):293-302. doi: 10.4103/1735-5362.189297.
2. Inocêncio Leite LH, Leite Gde O, Silva Coutinho T, de Sousa SD. Topical Antinociceptive Effect of Vanillosmopsis arborea Baker on Acute Corneal Pain in Mice. Evid Based Complement Alternat Med. 2014;2014:708636. doi: 10.1155/2014/708636. Epub 2014 Feb 10.

3. Sampaio Lde F, Maia JG, de Parijós AM, de Souza RZ, Barata LE. Linalool from rosewood (Aniba rosaeodora Ducke) oil inhibits adenylate cyclase in the retina, contributing to understanding its biological activity. Phytother Res. 2012 Jan;26(1):73-7. doi: 10.1002/ptr.3518. Epub 2011 May 5.
4. Adams MK, Sparrow JM, Jim S et al 2009 Inadvertent administration of Olbas oil into the eye: a surprisingly frequent presentation. Eye (London) 23:244
5. Peate WF 2007 Work-related eye injuries and illnesses. American Family Physician 75:1017-1022
6. Hillery A, Lloyd AW, Swarbick J. Drug Delivery and Targeting: For Pharmacists and Pharmaceutical Scientists. Available at: http://ajprd.com/downloadebooks_pdf/37.pdf. Last accessed February 15, 2017.

QUESTION 21
1. Bell KL. Holistic Aromatherapy for Animals: A Comprehensive Guide to the Use of Essential Oils & Hydrosols with Animals. 2002. Findhorn Press
2. Shelton M. The Animal Desk Reference. 2007. Essential Science Publishing.

QUESTION 22
1. Boa AN. Chemistry of Food. Available at: http://www.hull.ac.uk/php/chsanb/Food/Food_3.pdf. Last Accessed February 22, 2017.
2. The Accidental Scientist. Science of Cooking: Science of Eggs. Available at: https://www.exploratorium.edu/cooking/eggs/eggscience.html. Last Accessed February 22, 2017.
3. Turek C and Stintzing FC. Stability of Essential Oils. Comprehensive Reviews in Food Science and Food Safety.
4. Aravena G, García O, Muñoz O, Pérez-Correa JR, Parada J.The impact of cooking and delivery modes of thymol and carvacrol on retention and bioaccessibility in starchy foods.Food Chem. 2016 Apr 1;196:848-52. doi: 10.1016/j.foodchem.2015.09.099. Epub 2015 Oct 8.

QUESTION 23
1. Schnaubelt K. The Healing Intelligence of Essential Oils: The Science of Advanced Aromatherapy. Healing Arts Press. 2011
2. Tisserand R and Young R. Essential Oil Safety. 2nd ed. Churchill Livingston Elsevier. 2014
3. Buckle J. Clinical Aromatherapy: Essential Oils in Practice. 2nd ed. Churchill Livingstone. 2003.

QUESTION 24

1. Migraine: Symptoms and Causes. Mayo Clinic. Available at: http://www.mayoclinic.org/diseases-conditions/migraine-headache/symptoms-causes/dxc-20202434. Last Accessed: February 20, 2017.
2. Göbel H, Schmidt G, Dworschak M, Stolze H, Heuss D. Essential plant oils and headache mechanisms. Phytomedicine. 1995 Oct;2(2):93-102. doi: 10.1016/S0944-7113(11)80053-X.
3. Highlights of Prescribing Information. Imitrex (sumatriptan). GlaxoSmithKline. Available at: https://www.gsksource.com/pharma/content/dam/GlaxoSmithKline/US/en/Prescribing_Information/Imitrex_Tablets/pdf/IMITREX-TABLETS-PI-PIL.PDF. Last Accessed February 20, 2017.

QUESTION 25

1. Menon GK, Cleary GW, Lane ME. The structure and function of the stratum corneum. *International Journal of Pharmaceutics*. 2012;435(1):3-9.
2. Graham-Brown R, Burns T. *Lecture Notes: Dermatology*. 9th ed. Oxford, England: Wiley-Blackwell; 2007.
3. Jäger W, Buchbauer G, Jirovetz L, Fritzer M. Percutaneous absorption of lavender oil from a massage oil. J Soc Cosmet Chem. 1992. 43: 49-54 Available at: http://journal.scconline.org/pdf/cc1992/cc043n01/p00049-p00054.pdf. Last accessed February 26, 2017.
4. Mohammed D, Matts P, Hadgraft J, Lane M. Variation of stratum corneum biophysical and molecular properties with anatomic site. *AAPS Journal*. 2012;14(4):806-812.
5. Rougier A, Lotte C, Corcuff P, Maibach H. Relationship between skin permeability and corneocyte size according to anatomic site, age and sex in man. *J Soc Cosmet Chem*. 1988;39(1):15-26.
6. Kohlert C, Schindler G, Reinhard W, Abel G, Brinkhaus B, Derenforf H, Gräfe EU, Viet M. Systemic Availability and Pharmacokinetics of Thymol in Humans. J Clin Pharmaco. 2002;42:731-737.

QUESTION 26

1. Šošić-Jurjević B, Ajdžanović V, Filipović B, Trifunović S, et al. Functional morphology of pituitary -thyroid and -adrenocortical axes in middle-aged male rats treated with Vitex agnus castus essential oil. Acta Histochem. 2016 Sep;118(7):736-745. doi: 10.1016/j.acthis.2016.07.007

2. Sariözkan S, Türk G, Güvenç M, Yüce A, Özdamar S, Cantürk F, Yay AH. Effects of Cinnamon (C zeylanicum) Bark Oil Against Taxanes-Induced Damages In Sperm Quality, Testicular and Epididymal Oxidant/Antioxidant Balance, Testicular Apoptosis, and Sperm DNA Integrity. Nutr Cancer. 2016;68(3):481-94. doi: 10.1080/01635581.2016.1152384.

3. Saiyudthong S, Mekseepralard C. Effect of Inhaling Bergamot Oil on Depression-Related Behaviors in Chronic Stressed Rats. J Med Assoc Thai. 2015 Oct;98 Suppl 9:S152-9.

4. Deng XY, Xue JS, Li HY, Ma ZQ, et al. Geraniol produces antidepressant-like effects in a chronic unpredictable mild stress mice model. Physiol Behav. 2015 Dec 1;152(Pt A):264-71. doi: 10.1016/j.physbeh.2015.10.008.

5. Park HJ, Lim EJ, Zhao RJ, Oh SR, et al. Effect of the fragrance inhalation of essential oil from Asarum heterotropoides on depression-like behaviors in mice. BMC Complement Altern Med. 2015 Mar 6;15:43. doi: 10.1186/s12906-015-0571-1.

6. Sebai H, Selmi S, Rtibi K, Gharbi N, Sakly M. Protective Effect of Lavandula stoechas and Rosmarinus officinalis essential oils against reproductive damage and oxidative stress in alloxan-induced diabetic rats. J Med Food. 2015 Feb;18(2):241-9. doi: 10.1089/jmf.2014.0040.

7. Lee KB, Cho E, Kang YS. Changes in 5-hydroxytryptamine and cortisol plasma levels in menopausal women after inhalation of clary sage oil. Phytother Res. 2014 Nov;28(11):1599-605. doi: 10.1002/ptr.5163. Erratum in: Phytother Res. 2014 Dec;28(12):1897.

8. Politano VT, McGinty D, Lewis EM, Hoberman AM. Uterotrophic assay of percutaneous lavender oil in immature female rats. Int J Toxicol. 2013 Mar-Apr;32(2):123-9. doi: 10.1177/1091581812472209.

9. Tirabassi G, Giovannini L, Paggi F, Panin G et al. Possible efficacy of Lavender and Tea tree oils in the treatment of young women affected by mild idiopathic hirsutism. J Endocrinol Invest. 2013 Jan;36(1):50-4. doi: 10.3275/8766.

10. Fukada M, Kano E, Miyoshi M, Komaki R, et al. Effect of "rose essential oil" inhalation on stress-induced skin-barrier disruption in rats and humans. Chem Senses. 2012 May;37(4):347-56. doi: 10.1093/chemse/bjr108.

11. Köse E, Sarsilmaz M, Meydan S, Sönmez M, Kuş I, Kavakli A. The effect of lavender oil on serum testosterone levels and epididymal sperm characteristics of formaldehyde treated male rats. Eur Rev Med Pharmacol Sci. 2011 May;15(5):538-42.

12. Li YJ, Xuan HZ, Shou QY, Zhan ZG, Lu X, Hu FL. Therapeutic effects of propolis essential oil on anxiety of restraint-stressed mice. Hum Exp Toxicol. 2012 Feb;31(2):157-65. doi: 10.1177/0960327111412805.

13. Saiyudthong S, Marsden CA. Acute effects of bergamot oil on anxiety-related behaviour and corticosterone level in rats. Phytother Res. 2011 Jun;25(6):858-62. doi: 10.1002/ptr.3325.

14. Seol GH, Shim HS, Kim PJ, Moon HK. Antidepressant-like effect of Salvia sclarea is explained by modulation of dopamine activities in rats. J Ethnopharmacol. 2010 Jul 6;130(1):187-90. doi: 10.1016/j.jep.2010.04.035.

15. Seo JY. [The effects of aromatherapy on stress and stress responses in adolescents]. J Korean Acad Nurs. 2009 Jun;39(3):357-65. doi: 10.4040/jkan.2009.39.3.357. Article in Korean

16. Monti D, Tampucci S, Chetoni P, Burgalassi S. Niaouli oils from different sources: analysis and influence on cutaneous permeation of estradiol in vitro. Drug Deliv. 2009 Jul;16(5):237-42. doi: 10.1080/10717540902896297.

17. Diego M, Schanberg S, Kuhn C.Field T, Field T, Cullen C, Largie S. Lavender bath oil reduces stress and crying and enhances sleep in very young infants. Early Hum Dev. 2008 Jun;84(6):399-401.

18. Atsumi T, Tonosaki K. Smelling lavender and rosemary increases free radical scavenging activity and decreases cortisol level in saliva. Psychiatry Res. 2007 Feb 28;150(1):89-96.

19. Purves D, Augustine GJ, Fitzpatrick D, Katz LC, LaMantia AS, McNamara JO, Williams SM. Neuroscience, 2nd edition. Sunderland (MA): Sinauer Associates; 2001.

20. Howes MJ, Houghton PJ, Barlow DJ, Pocock VJ, Milligan SR. Assessment of estrogenic activity in some common essential oil constituents. J Pharm Pharmacol. 2002 Nov;54(11):1521-8.

QUESTION 27

1. Food Allergy Research and Education. Tree Nut Allergies. Available at: http://www.foodallergy.org/allergens/tree-nut-allerg y?gclid=CjwKEAiAtf6zBRDS0oCLrL37gFUSJACr2JYbyW4d5JoH ggZiEWmhqh_oXq-9TgjuzXzn22QP-iL01hoCSfjw_wcB. Accessed December 27, 2015.

2. Fries JH, Fries MW. Coconut: a review of its uses as they relate to the allergic individual. Ann Allergy 1983;51:472-81.

3. American Academy of Allergy, Asthma and Immunology (ACAAI), Tree Nut Allergy. Available at: http://www.acaai.org/allergist/ allergies/Types/food-allergies/types/Pages/tree-nut-allergy.aspx

4. Eigenmann PA, Burks AW, Bannon GA, et al. Identification of unique peanut and soy allergens in sera adsorbed with cross-reacting antibodies. J Allergy Clin Immunol 1996,90,969 70.

QUESTION 28

1. The Neurobiology of Drug Addiction. Definition of Tolerance. Available at: https://www.drugabuse.gov/publications/teaching-packets/neurobiology-drug-addiction/section-iii-action-heroin-morphine/6-definition-tolerance. Last Accessed: February 28, 2017.
2. Stern R. Can you Build a Tolerance to an Essential Oil? Available at: http://www.stitcher.com/podcast/dr-rory-f-stern/natural-healing-and-essential-oils/e/can-you-build-a-tolerance-to-an-essential-oil-39382405 . Last Accessed February 28, 2017.
3. Science Daily. Mechanism of signaling receptor recycling discovered. Available at: https://www.sciencedaily.com/releases/2010/12/101222112110.htm. Last Accessed February 28, 2017.

QUESTION 29

1. Rozas-Muñoza E,, Lepoittevin JP, Pujol RM, Giménez-Arnaua A. Allergic Contact Dermatitis to Plants: Understanding the Chemistry will Help our Diagnostic Approach. Actas Dermosifiliogr 2012;103:456-77 - Vol. 103 Num.6 DOI: 10.1016/j.adengl.2012.07.006
2. Schwartz L. Diagnosis of industrial skin diseases. Am J Public Health Nations Health, 1938: 28; 593-8
3. Cardullo AC, Ruszkowski AM, DeLeo VA. Allergic contact dermatitis resulting from sensitivity to citrus peel, geraniol, and citral. J Am Acad Dermatol, 1989: 21;395-7
4. Iziy E, Nasr SMB, Majd A Comparison of Allergenicity of Mature Pollen Grains and Petals in Two Ontogenic Stages in Cytisus scoparius L. J Biomed. 2016 June; 1(2):e5818.
5. Gardner Z, McGuffin M, eds. American Herbal Products Association's Botanical Safety Handbook, Second Edition.
6. Kurts G and Raraport MJ. External/internal allergy to plants (Artemesia). Contact Dermat. 1979: 5(5);407-409
7. Kurzen M, Bayerl C, and Goerdt S. Occupational allergy to mugwort. J Dtsch Dermatol Ges. 2003:1(4): 285-290
8. Rodrigues-Alves R, Pregal MC, Pereira-Santos MC et al. Anaphylasix to pine nut. Cross-reactivity to *Artmesia vulgaris*? Allergol Immunopathol. 2008;36(2):113-116

QUESTION 30

1. Farage MA. Perceptions of sensitive skin: changes in perceived severity and associations with environmental causes. Contact Dermatitis. 2008; 59: 226-232.
2. Pons-Guiraud A. Senssitive skin: a complex and multifactorial syndrome. J Cosmet Dermatol. 2004; 3: 145-148.
3. Farage MA, Katsorou A, Maibach HI. Sensory, clinical and physiological factors in sensitive skin: a review. Contact Dermatitis. 2006; 55: 1-14
4. Garg A, Chren MM, Sands LP. Psychological stress perrubs epidermal permeability barrier homeostasis: implication for the patholgenesis of stress-associated skin disorders. Arch Dermatol. 2001; 137: 53-59.
5. Tisserand R and Young R Essential Oil Safety: A Guide for Health Care Professionals 2nd ed. 2014. Elsevier Health Sciences.
6. Denda M, Tsuchiya T, Elias PM et al. Stress alters cutaneous permeability barrier homeostasis. Am J Physiol Regul Integr Comp Physiol. 2000; 237: R367-R372.
7. Saint-Mezard P, Chavagnac C, Bosset S, et al. Psychological stress exerts an adjuvant effect on skin dendritic cell function in vivo. J Immun. 2003. 171: 4073-4080.
8. Kawana S, Liang Z, Nagano M. Role of substance P in stress derived degranulation of dermal mast cells in mice. J Dermatol Sci. 2006. 42: 47.
9. Pollan M. In Defense of Food: An Eater's Manifesto. 2009. Penguin Books.

QUESTION 31

1. Jaggi, R. K., Madaan, R., and Singh, B. Anticonvulsant potential of holy basil, Ocimum sanctum Linn., and its cultures. Indian J Exp. Biol. 2003;41(11):1329-1333.
2. Sakina, M. R., Dandiya, P. C., Hamdard, M. E., and Hameed, A. Preliminary psychopharmacological evaluation of Ocimum sanctum leaf extract. J Ethnopharmacol. 1990;28(2):143-150.
3. Singh, S., Rehan, H. M., and Majumdar, D. K. Effect of Ocimum sanctum fixed oil on blood pressure, blood clotting time and pentobarbitone-induced sleeping time. J Ethnopharmacol. 2001;78(2-3):139-143.
4. Panda, S. and Kar, A. Ocimum sanctum leaf extract in the regulation of thyroid function in the male mouse. Pharmacol.Res 1998;38(2):107-110.

5. Ahmed, M., Ahamed, R. N., Aladakatti, R. H., and Ghosesawar, M. G. Reversible anti-fertility effect of benzene extract of Ocimum sanctum leaves on sperm parameters and fructose content in rats. J Basic Clin Physiol Pharmacol. 2002;13(1):51-59.

6. Kasinathan, S., Ramakrishnan, S., and Basu, S. L. Antifertility effect of Ocimum sanctum L. Indian J Exp.Biol. 1972;10(1):23-25.

7. Seth, S. D., Johri, N., and Sundaram, K. R. Antispermatogenic effect of Ocimum sanctum. Indian J Exp.Biol. 1981;19(10):975-976.

8. Vohora, S. B., Garg, S. K., and Chaudhury, R. R. Antifertility screening of plants. 3. Effect of six indigenous plants on early pregnancy in albino rats. Indian J Med Res 1969;57(5):893-899.

9. Buch, J. G., Dikshit, R. K., and Mansuri, S. M. Effect of certain volatile oils on ejaculated human spermatozoa. Indian J Med Res 1988;87:361-363.

10. Joshi, H. and Parle, M. Evaluation of nootropic potential of Ocimum sanctum Linn. in mice. Indian J Exp.Biol. 2006;44(2):133-136.

11. Moreira-Lobo, D. C., Linhares-Siqueira, E. D., Cruz, G. M., Cruz, J. S., Carvalho-de-Souza, J. L., Lahlou, S., Coelho-de-Souza, A. N., Barbosa, R., Magalhaes, P. J., and Leal-Cardoso, J. H. Eugenol modifies the excitability of rat sciatic nerve and superior cervical ganglion neurons. Neurosci.Lett. 3-26-2010;472(3):220-224.

12. Varney, E. and Buckle, J. Effect of inhaled essential oils on mental exhaustion and moderate burnout: a small pilot study. J Altern. Complement Med. 2013;19(1):69-71.

13. Saxena, R. C., Singh, R., Kumar, P., Negi, M. P., Saxena, V. S., Geetharani, P., Allan, J. J., and Venkateshwarlu, K. Efficacy of an Extract of Ocimum tenuiflorum (OciBest) in the Management of General Stress: A Double-Blind, Placebo-Controlled Study. Evid. Based.Complement Alternat. Med. 2012;2012:894509.

14. Bhattacharyya, D., Sur, T. K., Jana, U., and Debnath, P. K. Controlled programmed trial of Ocimum sanctum leaf on generalized anxiety disorders. Nepal. Med. Coll. J 2008;10(3):176-179.

15. Singh, S., Majumdar, D. K., and Rehan, H. M. Evaluation of anti-inflammatory potential of fixed oil of Ocimum sanctum (Holybasil) and its possible mechanism of action. J Ethnopharmacol. 1996;54(1):19-26.

16. Singh, S. Comparative evaluation of antiinflammatory potential of fixed oil of different species of Ocimum and its possible mechanism of action. Indian J Exp. Biol. 1998;36(10):1028-1031.

17. Singh, S., Majumdar, D. K., and Yadav, M. R. Chemical and pharmacological studies on fixed oil of *Ocimum sanctum*. Indian J Exp.Biol. 1996;34(12):1212-1215.
18. Godhwani, S., Godhwani, J. L., and Vyas, D. S. *Ocimum sanctum*: an experimental study evaluating its anti-inflammatory, analgesic and antipyretic activity in animals. J Ethnopharmacol. 1987;21(2):153-163.
19. Singh, S. and Majumdar, D. K. Effect of Ocimum sanctum fixed oil on vascular permeability and leucocytes migration. Indian J Exp. Biol. 1999;37(11):1136-1138.
20. Mediratta, P. K., Sharma, K. K., and Singh, S. Evaluation of immunomodulatory potential of Ocimum sanctum seed oil and its possible mechanism of action. J Ethnopharmacol. 2002;80(1):15-20.
21. Jagetia, G. C. and Baliga, M. S. The evaluation of nitric oxide scavenging activity of certain Indian medicinal plants in vitro: a preliminary study. J Med Food 2004;7(3):343-348.
22. Kelm, M. A., Nair, M. G., Strasburg, G. M., and DeWitt, D. L. Antioxidant and cyclooxygenase inhibitory phenolic compounds from Ocimum sanctum Linn. Phytomedicine. 2000;7(1):7-13.
23. Yanpallewar, S. U., Rai, S., Kumar, M., and Acharya, S. B. Evaluation of antioxidant and neuroprotective effect of *Ocimum sanctum* on transient cerebral ischemia and long-term cerebral hypoperfusion. Pharmacol.Biochem.Behav. 2004;79(1):155-164.
24. Tohti, I., Tursun, M., Umar, A., Turdi, S., Imin, H., and Moore, N. Aqueous extracts of Ocimum basilicum L. (sweet basil) decrease platelet aggregation induced by ADP and thrombin in vitro and rats arterio--venous shunt thrombosis in vivo. Thromb.Res 2006;118(6):733-739.
25. Tognolini, M., Barocelli, E., Ballabeni, V., Bruni, R., Bianchi, A., Chiavarini, M., and Impicciatore, M. Comparative screening of plant essential oils: phenylpropanoid moiety as basic core for antiplatelet activity. Life Sci. 2-23-2006;78(13):1419-1432.
26. Amrani, S., Harnafi, H., Gadi, D., Mekhfi, H., Legssyer, A., Aziz, M., Martin-Nizard, F., and Bosca, L. Vasorelaxant and anti-platelet aggregation effects of aqueous *Ocimum basilicum* extract. J Ethnopharmacol. 8-17-2009;125(1):157-162.
27. Broadhurst, C. L., Polansky, M. M., and Anderson, R. A. Insulin-like biological activity of culinary and medicinal plant aqueous extracts in vitro. J Agric.Food Chem 2000;48(3):849-852.
28. Umar, A., Imam, G., Yimin, W., Kerim, P., Tohti, I., Berke, B., and Moore, N. Antihypertensive effects of *Ocimum basilicum* L. (OBL) on blood pressure in renovascular hypertensive rats. Hypertens. Res 5-7-2010

29. Bravo, E., Amrani, S., Aziz, M., Harnafi, H., and Napolitano, M. Ocimum basilicum ethanolic extract decreases cholesterol synthesis and lipid accumulation in human macrophages. Fitoterapia 2008;79(7-8):515-523

QUESTION 32

1. Adefegha SA, Olasehinde TA, Oboh G. Essential Oil Composition, Antioxidant, Antidiabetic and Antihypertensive Properties of Two Afromomum Species. J Oleo Sci. 2017 Jan 1;66(1):51-63. doi: 10.5650/jos.ess16029. Epub 2016 Dec 8.

2. Ferreira, A.C.F.; Neto, J.C.; Silva, A.C.M.; Kuster, R.M.; Carvalho, D.P. Inhibition of thyroid peroxidase by *Myrcia uniflora* flavonoids. Chem. Res. Toxicol. 2006, 19, 351–355.

3. Mnafgui K, Kchaou M, Ben Salah H, Hajji R, et al. Essential oil of Zygophyllum album inhibits key-digestive enzymes related to diabetes and hypertension and attenuates symptoms of diarrhea in alloxan-induced diabetic rats. Pharm Biol. 2016 Aug;54(8):1326-33. doi: 10.3109/13880209.2015.1075049. Epub 2015 Oct 6.

4. Małachowska B, Fendler W, Pomykała A, Suwała S, Młynarski W. Essential oils reduce autonomous response to pain sensation during self-monitoring of blood glucose among children with diabetes. J Pediatr Endocrinol Metab. 2016 Jan;29(1):47-53. doi: 10.1515/jpem-2014-0361.

5. Oboh G, Akinbola IA, Ademosun AO, Sanni DM. Essential Oil from Clove Bud (*Eugenia aromatica* Kuntze) Inhibit Key Enzymes Relevant to the Management of Type-2 Diabetes and Some Pro-oxidant Induced Lipid Peroxidation in Rats Pancreas in vitro. J Oleo Sci. 2015;64(7):775-82. doi: 10.5650/jos.ess14274. Epub 2015 May 21.

6. Sheikh BA, Pari L, Rathinam A, Chandramohan R.Trans-anethole, a terpenoid ameliorates hyperglycemia by regulating key enzymes of carbohydrate metabolism in streptozotocin induced diabetic rats. Biochimie. 2015 May;112:57-65. doi: 10.1016/j.biochi.2015.02.008. Epub 2015 Feb 20.

7. Hasanein P, Riahi H. Antinociceptive and antihyperglycemic effects of *Melissa officinalis* essential oil in an experimental model of diabetes. Med Princ Pract. 2015;24(1):47-52. doi: 10.1159/000368755.

8. Akolade JO, Usman LA, Okereke OE, Muhammad NO. Antidiabetic potentials of essential oil extracted from the leaves of *Hoslundia opposita* Vahl. J Med Food. 2014 Oct;17(10):1122-8. doi: 10.1089/jmf.2013.0118. Epub 2014 Aug 19.

9. Sebai H, Selmi S, Rtibi K, Souli A, et al. Lavender (Lavandula stoechas L.) essential oils attenuate hyperglycemia and protect against oxidative stress in alloxan-induced diabetic rats. Lipids Health Dis. 2013 Dec 28;12:189. doi: 10.1186/1476-511X-12-189.
10. Ganiyu Oboh, Ayokunle O. Ademosun, Oluwatoyin V. Odubanjo, and Ifeoluwa A. Akinbola, Antioxidative Properties and Inhibition of Key Enzymes Relevant to Type-2 Diabetes and Hypertension by Essential Oils from Black Pepper. Advances in Pharmacological Sciences, 2013, Article ID 926047, 6 pages, 2013. doi:10.1155/2013/926047
11. Joo HE, Lee HJ, Sohn EJ, Lee MH, Ko HS, Jeong SJ, Lee HJ, Kim SH. Anti-diabetic potential of the essential oil of Pinus koraiensis leaves toward streptozotocin-treated mice and HIT-T15 pancreatic β cells. Biosci Biotechnol Biochem. 2013;77(10):1997-2001.
12. Kim Y, Keogh JB, Clifton PM. Polyphenols and Glycemic Control. Nutrients. 2016 Jan 5;8(1). pii: E17. doi: 10.3390/nu8010017.
13. Motilal S, Maharaj RG. Nutmeg extracts for painful diabetic neuropathy: a randomized, double-blind, controlled study. J Altern Complement Med. 2013 Apr;19(4):347-52. doi: 10.1089/ acm.2012.0016. Epub 2012 Oct 25.
14. Davis PA, Yokoyama W. Cinnamon intake lowers fasting blood glucose: meta-analysis. J Med Food. 2011 Sep;14(9):884-9. doi: 10.1089/jmf.2010.0180. Epub 2011 Apr 11.

QUESTION 33

1. Code of Federal Regulations, 40: Chapter 1, Subchapter C, Part 51, Subpart F, 51100. Last accessed 18 February 2017, and EPA's Terms of Environment Glossary, Abbreviations, and Acronyms.
2. Farrow A, Taylor H, Northstone K et al. Symptoms of mothers and infants related to total volatile organic compounds in household products. Arch Environ Health. 2003. 58:633-641.
3. Millqvist Ternesten-Hasséus E, Ståhl A, et al. Changes in levels of nerve growth factor in nasal secretions after capsaicin inhalation in patients with airway symptoms from scents and chemicals. Environ Health Perspect. 2005. 113: 849-852.
4. Steinhagen WH and Barrow CS. Sensory irritation structure-activity of inhaled aldehydes in B6C3F1 and Swiss-Webster mice. Toxicol Appl Pharmacol.1984. 72:495-503.
5. Luan HF, Ma W, Zhang, X, et al. Quantitative structure-activity relationship models for prediction of sensory irritants (log RD50) of volatile organic chemicals. Chemosphere. 2006. 63(7):1142-1153. Available at: http://www.sciencedirect.com/science/article/pii/S0045653505011471. Last Accessed February 21, 2017.

6   Lamorena RB, Jung SG, Bae GN, et al. The formation of ultrafine particle during ozone-initiated oxidations with terpenes emitted from natural paint. J Hazard Mater. 2007 141:245-251. Available at: https://www.ncbi.nlm.nih.gov/pubmed/16908097. Last accessed February 21, 2017.

7. Wolkoff P, Clausen PA, Larsen K, et al.. Acute airway effects of ozone-initiated d-limonene chemistry: Importance of gaseous products Toxicology Letters 2008. 181(3):171-6

8. Hedenstierna, G., Alexandersson, R., Wimander, K. et al. Int. Arch Occup Environ Heath. 1983. 51: 191. doi:10.1007/BF00377751

9. Norbäck D, Björnsson E, Janson C, et al. Asthmatic symptoms and volatile organic compounds, formaldehyde, and carbon dioxide in dwellings. Occupational and Environmental Medicine 1995;52:388-395. Available at: http://oem.bmj.com/content/52/6/388. Last Accessed: February 21, 2017.

10. Låstbom L, Boman A, Johnsson S, Camner P, Ryrfeldt A. Increased airway responsiveness of a common fragrance component, 3-carene, after skin sensitisation--a study in isolated guinea pig lungs. Toxicol Lett. 2003 Nov 30;145(2):189-96. Available at: https://www.ncbi.nlm.nih.gov/pubmed/14581172. Last accessed February 21, 2017.

11. Låstbom L, Boman A, Camner P, Ryrfeldt A. Increased airway responsiveness after skin sensitisation to 3-carene, studied in isolated guinea pig lungs. Toxicology. 2000 Jul 5;147(3):209-14. Available at: https://www.ncbi.nlm.nih.gov/pubmed/10924802. Last Accessed February 21, 2017.

12. Låstbom L, Boman A, Camner P, Ryrfeldt A. Does airway responsiveness increase after skin sensitisation to 3-carene: a study in isolated guinea pig lungs. Toxicology. 1998 Jan 16;125(1):59-66. Available at: https://www.ncbi.nlm.nih.gov/pubmed/9585101. Last Accessed February 21, 2017.

13. Nielsen GD, Larsen ST, Olsen O, Løvik M, Poulsen LK, Glue C, Wolkoff P. Do indoor chemicals promote development of airway allergy? Indoor Air. 2007 Jun;17(3):236-55. Available at: https://www.ncbi.nlm.nih.gov/pubmed/17542836. Last Accessed February 21, 2017.

14. Nielsen GD1, Wolkoff P, Alarie Y. Sensory irritation: risk assessment approaches. Regul Toxicol Pharmacol. 2007 Jun;48(1):6-18. Epub 2007 Jan 22.

15. Hilton I, Dearman RJ, Fielding I, et al. Evaluation of the sensitizing potential of eugenol and isoeugenol in mice and guinea pigs. J Appl Toxicol. 1996. 16: 459-464. Available at: https://www.ncbi.nlm.nih.gov/pubmed/8889799. Last Accessed February 21, 2017.

16. Schnuch A, Oppel E, Oppel T et al. Experimental inhalation of fragrance allergens in predisposed subjects: effects on skin and airways. Br J Dermatol 2011. 162: 598-602.

17. Masamoto Y, Kawabata F, Fushiki T. Intragastric administration of TRPV1, TRPV3, TRPV8, TRPA1 agonists modulates autonomic thermoregulation. Biosci Biotechnol Biochem. 2009 May;73(5):1021-7. Epub 2009 May 7. Available at: https://www.ncbi.nlm.nih.gov/pubmed/19420725. Last Accessed February 21, 2017.

18. Canning BJ, Farmer DG, Mori N. Mechanistic studies of acid evoked coughing in anesthetized guinea pigs. Am J Physiol Regul Integr Comp Physioil. 2006. 291: R454-463. Available at: https://www.ncbi.nlm.nih.gov/labs/articles/16914432/. Last Accessed February 21, 2017.

19. André E, Camp B, Materazzi S, et al. Cigarette smoke-induced neurogenic inflammation is mediated by α,β-unsaturated aldehydes and the TRPA1 receptor in rodents. J Clin Invest. 2008. 118:2574-2582. Available at: https://www.ncbi.nlm.nih.gov/pubmed/18568077. Last Accessed: February 21, 2017.

20. Hasani A, Pavia D, Toms N et al. Effect of aromatics on lung mucociliary clearance in patients with chronic airways obstruction. J Altern Complement. Med. 2003. 9:243-249. Available at: http://online.liebertpub.com/doi/abs/10.1089/10755530360623356. Last Accessed February 21, 2017.

21. Bessac BF and Jordt SE. Breathtaking TRP channels: TRPA1 and TRPV1 in airway chemosensation and reflex control. Physiol. 2008. 23: 360-370.

22. Stotz SC, Vrients J, Martyn D, et al. Citral sensing by TRANSient receptor potential channels in dorsal root ganglion neurons. PLoS ONE. 2008. 3(5), e2082.

23. Mandadi S, Nakanishi ST, Takashima Y et al. Locomotor networks are targets of modulation by sensory transient receptor potential vanilloid 1 and transient receptor potential melastatin 8 channels. Neuroscience. 2009: 162, 1377-1397

24. Lee SP, Buber MT, Yang Q, et al. Thymol and related alkyl phenols activate that hTRPA1channel. Br J Pharmacol. 2008. 153:1739-1749. Available at: https://www.ncbi.nlm.nih.gov/pubmed/18334983. Last Accessed February 21, 2017.

25. Schäfer D and Schäfer W. Pharmacological studies with an ointment containing menthol, camphene, and essential oils for broncholytic and secretolytic effects. Arzneimittelforchung. 1981. 31: 82-86. Available at: https://www.ncbi.nlm.nih.gov/pubmed/7194098. Last Accessed February 21, 2017.

26. Chronic obstructive pulmonary disease in over 16s: diagnosis and management. Available at: https://www.nice.org.uk/guidance/CG101/chapter/introduction. Last accessed February 17, 2017.
27. GOLD 2017 Global Strategy for the Diagnosis, Management and Prevention of COPD. Available at: http://goldcopd.org/gold-2017-global-strategy-diagnosis-management-prevention-copd/. Last Accessed February 17, 2017.
28. Qaseem A, Wilt TJ, Weinberger SE, Hania NA et al. Diagnosis and Management of Stable Chronic Obstructive Pulmonary Disease: A Clinical Practice Guideline update from The American College of Physicians, American College of Chest Physicians, American Thoracic Society, and European Respiratory Society. Available at: https://www.thoracic.org/statements/resources/copd/179full.pdf. Last Accessed February 17, 2017.
29. Healthy Environments. Substances that Lead to Asthma. Available at: https://nems.nih.gov/Sustainability/Documents/NIH%20Asthma%20Report.pdf. Last Accessed February 17, 2017.
30. Hoffman LR, Yen E, et al. Lipoid pneumonia due to Mexican folk remedy. Arch Pediatr Adolesc Med. 2005; 159:11.
31. Costa, et al. Exogenous lipoid pneumonia—a case report. Rev Port Pneumol. 2005;11(6):567–72 (Nov–Dec).
32. Chaveau M., et al. Exogenous lipoid pneumonia: a simple diagnosis? Rev Med Liege. 2005;60(10):799–804 (Oct).
33. Gondouin A, Manzoni P, et al. Exogenous lipoid pneumonia: a retrospective multicentre study of 44 cases in France. Eur Respir J 1996;9(7):1463–9 (Jul).
34. Bhagat R, Holmes IH, et al. Self-Injection with olive oil. A cause of lipoid pneumonia. Chest. 1995;107(3):875–6 (Mar).
35. Hirata M, Morita M, Maebou A, Hara H, Yoshimoto T, Hirao F. A case of exogenous lipoid pneumonia probably due to domestic insecticide. Nihon Kyobu Shikkan Gakkai Zasshi. 1993;31(10):1317–21 (Oct).
36. Alaminos Garcia P, Colodro Ruiz A, Menduina Guillen MJ, Banez Sanchez F, Perez Chica G. Exogenous lipoid pneumonia. Presentation of a new case. An Med Interna. 2005;22(6):283–4 (Jun).
37. Mydlowski T, Malong P, Wiatr E. Exogenous lipoid pneumonia— case report. Pneumonol Alergol Pol. 2004;72(5–6):214–6.
38. Brown AC, Slocum PC, Putthoff SL, Wallace WE, Foresman BH. Exogenous lipoid pneumonia due to nasal application of petroleum jelly. Chest. 1994;105(3):968–9 (Mar).
39. Dawson JK, Abernethy VE, Graham DR, Lynch MP. A woman who took cod-liver oil and smoked. Lancet. 1996;347(9018):1804 (Jun 29).

40. M. Doubkováa, M. Doubekb, M. Moulisc, J, et al. Exogenous lipoid pneumonia caused by chronic improper use of baby body oil in adult patient. Sociedade Portuguesa de Pneumologia. 2012. Available at: http://www.elsevier.pt/en/revistas/revista-portuguesa-pneumologia-320/artigo/exogenous-lipoid-pneumonia-caused-by-chronic-improper-use-S0873215913000561. Last Accessed February 17, 2017.

41. Bouti K, Rhorfi I.A., Mzouri M, Abid A, Alaoui Tahiri K. Exogenous lipoid pneumonia caused by *Nigella sativa* oil – A case report. Egyptian Journal of Chest Diseases and Tuberculosis. 2013. 62(4): 701–704

42. Betancourt SL, Martinez-Jimenez S, Rossi SE, Truong MT, Carrillo J, Erasmus JJ. Lipoid Pneumonia: Spectrum of Clinical and Radiologic Manifestations. Am J Roentgenology. 2010 194(1). Available at: http://www.ajronline.org/doi/full/10.2214/AJR.09.3040. Last Accessed February 17, 2017.

43. Indumathi CK, Vikram Kumar S, Paul P and Lewin S. Severe Lipoid Pneumonia Following Aspiration of Machine Oil: Successful Treatment with Steroids. Indian J Chest Dis Allied Sci 2012;54:197-199

44. Franck Rahaghi, Ali Varasteh, Roya Memarpour, and Basheer Tashtoush, Teppanyaki/Hibachi Pneumonitis: An Exotic Cause of Exogenous Lipoid Pneumonia," Case Reports in Pulmonology, vol. 2016, Article ID 1035601, 5 pages, 2016. doi:10.1155/2016/1035601

45. Hotta T, Tsubata Y, Okimoto T, Hoshino T, Hamaguchi S, Isobe T. Exogenous lipoid pneumonia caused by herbicide inhalation. Respirology Case Reports, 4 (5), 2016, e00172

46. Brown C. Endogenous Lipid Pneumonia in Opossums from Louisiana. Journal of Wildlife Diseases. 1988. 24(2): pp. 214-21

47. Buda P, Wieteska-Klimczak A, Własienko A, Mazur A, Ziołkowski J, Jaworska J, Kościesza A, Dunin-Wąsowicz D, Książyk J. Lipoid pneumonia — a case of refractory pneumonia in a child treated with ketogenic diet. Praca wpłynęła do Redakcji: 2013. 19.11.2012 r. [Article in Polish]

48. Venkatnarayan K, Madan K, Walia R, Kumar Jaya, Jain D, Guleria R "Diesel siphoner's lung": Exogenous lipoid pneumonia following hydrocarbon aspiration. Lung India. 2014. 31(1):63-66

49. Nicholson AG, Wells AU, Hooper J, Hansell DM, Kelleher A, and Morgan C. Successful Treatment of Endogenous Lipoid Pneumonia due to Niemann–Pick Type B Disease with Whole-Lung Lavage. American Journal of Respiratory and Critical Care Medicine. 2002. 165(1). DOI: http://dx.doi.org/10.1164/ajrccm.165.1.2103113

50. Tamura A, Hebisawa A, Fukushima K, Yotsumoto H, Mori M. Lipoid Pneumonia in Lung Cancer: Radiographic and Pathological Features. *Jpn J Clin Oncol* 1998; 28 (8): 492-496. doi: 10.1093/jjco/28.8.492

51. Hui C-K. Endogenous lipoid pneumonia associated with Legionella pneumophila serogroup 1. Singapore Med J 2013; 54(3): e66-e67.

52. McCauley L, Markin C, Hosmer D. An unexpected consequence of electronic cigarette use. Chest. 2012 Apr;141(4):1110-3. doi: 10.1378/chest.11-1334.

53. Decocq G, Dol L, Leroy D et al. Lipid pneumonia after aerosol therapy with gomenol in a 4 month old child. Presse Méd. 1996. (25): 994-995.

54. CF Foundation Recommends Against Using Peppermint Oil in Nebulizer. Available at: https://www.cff.org/News/News-Archive/2014/CF-Foundation-Recommends-Against-Using-Peppermint-Oil-in-Nebulizer/ Last Accessed February 17, 2017.

55. Hartley J. *Pseudomonas* a. in the Cystic Fibrosis Lung: The Inhibition of Bio-encapsulated Pathogens. [Abstract] Available at: http://www.csef.colostate.edu/2013_Abstracts/Hartley_Jenna.pdf. Accessed February 17, 2017.

QUESTION 34

1. Zhou HL, Deng YM, Xie QM. The modulatory effects of the volatile oil of ginger on the cellular immune response in vitro and in vivo in mice. J Ethnopharmacol. 2006 Apr 21;105(1-2):301-5. Epub 2005 Dec 9.

2. Su JY, Luo X, Zhang XJ, Deng XL, et al. Immunosuppressive activity of pogostone on T cells: Blocking proliferation via S phase arrest. Int Immunopharmacol. 2015 Jun;26(2):328-37. doi: 10.1016/j.intimp.2015.04.019.

3. Rezapour-Firouzi S, Arefhosseini SR, Mehdi F, Mehrangiz EM, et al. Immunomodulatory and therapeutic effects of Hot-nature diet and co-supplemented hemp seed, evening primrose oils intervention in multiple sclerosis patients. Complement Ther Med. 2013 Oct;21(5):473-80. doi: 10.1016/j.ctim.2013.06.006.

4. [No authors listed]. Retraction. Effects of thymoquinone (volatile oil of black cumin) on rheumatoid arthritis in rat models. Phytother Res. 2015 Mar;29(3):474. doi: 10.1002/ptr.5312.

5. Belch JJ, Hill A. Evening primrose oil and borage oil in rheumatologic conditions. Am J Clin Nutr. 2000 Jan;71(1 Suppl):352S-6S. Review.

6. Harbige LS. Dietary n-6 and n-3 fatty acids in immunity and autoimmune disease. Proc Nutr Soc. 1998 Nov;57(4):555-62. Review.
7. Horrobin DF. Essential fatty acid and prostaglandin metabolism in Sjögren's syndrome, systemic sclerosis and rheumatoid arthritis. Scand J Rheumatol Suppl. 1986;61:242-5. Review.
8. Berraaouan A, Abid S, Bnouham M. Antidiabetic oils. Curr Diabetes Rev. 2013 Nov;9(6):499-505. Review.
9. Krishna Mohan I, Das UN. Prevention of chemically induced diabetes mellitus in experimental animals by polyunsaturated fatty acids. Nutrition. 2001 Feb;17(2):126-51.
10. Pazyar N, Yaghoobi R. Tea tree oil as a novel antipsoriasis weapon. Skin Pharmacol Physiol. 2012;25(3):162-3. doi: 10.1159/000337936. Epub 2012 Apr 3.
11. Walsh D. Using aromatherapy in the management of psoriasis. Nurs Stand. 1996 Dec 18;11(13-15):53-6.

QUESTION 35

1. GERD Diseases and Conditions. Mayo Clinic. Available at: http://www.mayoclinic.org/diseases-conditions/gerd/basics/definition/con-20025201. Last Accessed February 13, 2017.
2. Jarosz M and Taraszewska A. Risk factors for gastroesophageal reflux disease: the role of diet. Prz Gastroenterol. 2014;9(5):297-301. doi: 10.5114/pg.2014.46166. Epub 2014 Oct 19.
3. Inamori M, Akiyama T, Akimoto K, et al. Early effects of peppermint oil on gastric emptying: a crossover study using a continuous real-time 13C breath test (BreathID system). J Gastroenterol 2007;42:539-542.
4. Patrick L. Gastroesophageal Reflux Disease (GERD): A Review of Conventional and Alternative Treatments. Alternative Medicine Reviews. 2011. 16(2)116-133.

QUESTION 36

1. Franchomme P, Pénöel D L'aromathérapie exactement. 1990 Jollois, Limoges
2. Topçu G, Gören AC 2007 Biological activity of diterpenoids isolated from Anatolian Lamiaceae plants. Records of Natural Products 1:1-16.
3. Henly DV, Lipson N, Korach K, Bloch CA. Prepubertal Gynecomastia Linked to Lavender and Tea Tree Oils. N Engl J Med 2007; 356:479-485. Available at: http://www.nejm.org/doi/full/10.1056/NEJMoa064725. Last accessed February 17, 2017.

4. Carson C, Tisserand R, Larkman T. Lack of evidence that essential oils affect puberty. Reproductive Toxicology. 2011. 44: 50-51
5. Tisserand R and Young R Essential Oil Safety: A Guide for Health Care Professionals 2nd ed. 2014. Elsevier Health Sciences.
6. Kemper KJ, et al; Kalyan S; Kutz JL; Dean CJ. Correspondence. Prepubertal Gynecomastic Linked to Lavender and Tea Tree Oils. N Engl J Med 2007; 356:2541-2544. Available at: http://www. nejm.org/doi/full/10.1056/NEJMoa064725#t=articleTop. Last accessed February 17, 2017.
7. Sashidhara KV, Rosaiah JN, Kumar A 2007 Cell growth inhibitory action of an unusual labdane diterpene, 13-epi-sclareol in breast and uterine cancers in vitro. Phytotherapy Research 21:1105-1108
8. Tisserand R. Is clary sage estrogenic? Available at: http:// roberttisserand.com/2010/04/is-clary-sage-oil-estrogenic/. Last accessed February 13, 2017.
9. Tabanca N, Khan SI, Bedir E, et al. Estrogenic activitiy of isolated compounds and essential oils of Pimpinella species from Turkey, evaluated using a recombinant yeast screen. Planta Med. 2004. 70: 728-735
10. Zondek B and Bergman E. Phenol methyl esters as estrogenic agents. Biochem J. 1938. 32:641-645
11. Nishihara T, Nishkawa J, Kanayama T et al. Estrogenic activities of 517 chemical sby yeast two-hybrid assay. J Health Sci. 2000. 46:282-298.
12. Jordan VC. Estrogen/antiestrogen Action and Breast Cancer Therapy. 1986. Univ of Wisconsin Press. pp. 21–22. ISBN 978-0-299-10480-1.
13. Melzig MF, Moller I, Jarry H. New investigations of the in vitro pharmacological activity of essential oils from the Apiaceae. Zeitschrift für Phytotherapie. 2003, 24, 112-116.

QUESTION 37

1. Tisserand, R and Rodney Young. Essential Oil Safety: A Guide for Health Care Professionals. 2nd ed. 2013. Churchill-Livingstone.
2. Valnet J. Aromatherapie. 1964. Librarie Maloine, Paris. (English translation. Valnet J. The practice of aromatherapy. 1990. CW Daniel.)
3. Caujolle F and Franck C. Sur l'action pharmacodynamique de l'essence d'hysop. Comptes Rendues Société Biologique. 1945. 139:1111.
4. Caujolle F and Franck C. On the pharmacodynamics action of lavender, lavandin, and spike lavender oils. Ann Pharm Fr. 1944. 2: 147-148.

5. Caujolle F and Franck C. Pharmacodynamic actions of clary sage and condiment sage. Competes Rendues Société Biologique. 1945. 139: 1109-1110.
6. Coombs HC and Pike FH. Respiratory and cardiovascular changes in the cat during conulsions of experimental origin. Am J Physiol. 1931. 97:92-106.
7. Freeman R. Cardiovascular manifestation of autonomic epilepsy. Clin Auton Res. 2006. 16: 12-17.
8. Hamden K, Keskes H, Belhaj S. Inhibitory potential of omega-3 fatty and fenugreek essential oil on key enzymes of carbohydrate-digestion and hypertension in diabetes rats. Lipids Health Dis. 2011. 10:226
9. Shiina Y, Funabashi N, Lee K, et al. Relaxation effects of lavender aromatherapy improve coronary flow velocity reserve in healthy men evaluated by transthoracic Doppler echocardiography. Int J Cardiol. 2008. 129: 193-197.
10. Dayawansa S, Umeno K, Takakura H, et al. Autonomic responses during inhalation of natural fragrance of cedrol in humans. Auton Neurosci. 2003. 108: 79-86.
11. Haze S, Sakai S, Gozu Y. Effects of fragrance inhalation on sympathetic activity in normal adults. Jpn J Pharmacol. 2002. 90: 247-253.
12. Barrie SA, Wright JV, Pizzorno JE. Effects of garlic oil on platelet aggregation, serum lipids, and blood pressure in humans. J Orthomol Med. 1987. 2(1): 15-21.
13. Zhang XH, Lowe D, Giles P. A randomized trial of the effects of garlic oil upon cardiovascular risk factors in trained male runners. Blood Coagul Fibrinolysis. 2001. 12: 67-74.
14. Lahlou S, Magalhaes PJ, de Siqueira RJ et al. Cardiovascular effects of the essential oils of Aniba canelilla bark in normotensive rats. J Cardiovasc Pharmacol. 2005. 46: 412-421
15. Hongratanaworakit T, Buchbauer G. Evaluation of the harmonizing effects of ylang-ylang oil on humans after inhalation. Plant Med. 2004. 70:632-636.
16. Magyar J, Szentandrassy N, Banyasz T et al. Effects of terpenoid phenol derivatives on calcium current in canine and human ventricular cardiomyocytes. Eur J Pharmacol. 2004. 487:29-36.
17. Northover BJ, Verghese J. The pharmacology of certain terpene alcohols and oxides. J Sci Industrial Res. 1962. 21C: 342-345.
18. Rakieten N, Rakieten ML. The effect of l-menthol on the systemic blood pressure. J Am Pharm Assoc. 1957. 46(2): 82-84.

19. Hypertensive Crisis: When You Should Call 9 1 1 for High Blood Pressure. Am Heart Ass. 2016. Available at: http://www.heart.org/HEARTORG/Conditions/HighBloodPressure/LearnHowHBPHarmsYourHealth/How-High-Blood-Pressure-Can-Lead-to-Stroke_UCM_301824_Article.jsp#.WJtYPxDwj4V. Last accessed February 8, 2017.
20. Spot a Stroke FAST. Am Heart Ass. Am Stroke Ass. 2017. Available at: http://www.strokeassociation.org/STROKEORG/WarningSigns/Stroke-Warning-Signs-and-Symptoms_UCM_308528_SubHomePage.jsp. Last accessed February 8, 2017.

QUESTION 38

1. Cassella JP, Cassella S, Ashford RL. Use of essential oil therapies in immunocompromised patients. J Antimicrob Chemother (2000) 45 (4): 550-551.
2. Juergens, U. R., Stober, M. & Vetter, H. Inhibition of cytokine production and arachidonic acid metabolism by eucalyptol (1,8-cineole) in human blood monocytes in vitro. European Journal of Medical Research 1998. 3: 508–10.
3. Loizzo MR, Tundis R, Menichini F, Saab AM, Statti GA, Menichini F. Cytotoxic activity of essential oils from labiatae and lauraceae families against in vitro human tumor models. Anticancer Res. 2007 Sep-Oct;27(5A):3293-9.
4. Aromatherapy and Essential Oils. PDQ Integrative, Alternative and Complementary Therapies Editorial Board. Available at: https://www.ncbi.nlm.nih.gov/pubmedhealth/PMH0032518/. Last accessed February 13, 2017.
5. Ndao DH, Ladas EJ, Cheng B, Sands SA, Snyder KT, Garvin JH Jr, Kelly KM. Inhalation aromatherapy in children and adolescents undergoing stem cell infusion: results of a placebo-controlled double-blind trial. Psychooncology. 2012 Mar;21(3):247-54. doi: 10.1002/pon.1898. Epub 2010 Dec 27.
6. Tate S. Peppermint oil: a treatment for postoperative nausea. J Adv Nurs. 1997 Sep;26(3):543-9.
7. Potter P, Eisenberg S, Cain KC, et al.: Orange interventions for symptoms associated with dimethyl sulfoxide during stem cell reinfusions: a feasibility study. Cancer Nurs 34 (5): 361-8, 2011 Sep-Oct.
8. Kite SM, Maher EJ, Anderson K, et al.: Development of an aromatherapy service at a Cancer Centre. Palliat Med 12 (3): 171-80, 1998.

QUESTION 39

1. Blashke T and Bjornsson T. Pharmacokinetics and pharmacoepidemiology. Scientific American. 1995. 8:1-14
2. Albert-Puleo M. Fennel and Anise as Estrogenic Agents. J Ethnopharmacol. 1980. 2(4):337-344
3. Buckle J. Clinical Aromatherapy: Essential Oils in Practice. 2nd ed. Churchill Livingstone. 2003.
4. Tisserand R and Young R. Essential Oil Safety. 2nd ed. Churchill Livingston Elsevier. 2014
5. Liston HL, Markowitz JS, DeVane CL. Drug glucuronidation in clinical psychopharmacology. J Clin Psychopharmacol. 2001. 21 (5): 500–15. doi:10.1097/00004714-200110000-00008. PMID 11593076.
6. Boyland E, Chasseaud LF. The role of glutathione and glutathione S-transferases in mercapturic acid biosynthesis. Adv. Enzymol. Relat. Areas Mol. Biol. Advances in Enzymology – and Related Areas of Molecular Biology. 1969. 32: 173–219. doi:10.1002/9780470122778.ch5. ISBN 9780470122778. PMID 4892500.
7. United States Food and Drug Administration. Drug Development and Drug Interactions: Table of Substrates, Inducers and Inhibitors. Available at: https://www.fda.gov/drugs/developmentapprovalprocess/developmentresources/druginteractionslabeling/ucm093664.htm. Last Accessed February 22, 2017.
8. Yip AS, Chow WH, Tai YT. Adverse effect of topical methyl salicylate ointment on warfarin anticoagulation: an unrecognized potential hazard. Postgrad. Med. 1990. 66: 367-369.
9. Chow WH, Cheung KL, Ling HM. See, T. Potentiation of warfarin anticoagulation by topical methylsalicylate ointment. J R Soc Med. 1989. 82:501-502.
10. Wang K and Su CY. Pharmacokinetics and disposition of beta-elemene in rats. Yoa Xue Xue Bao. 2000. 35: 725-728.
11. Lehman-Mckeeman LD, Rodriguez PA, Takigiku R, et al. d-Limonene-induced male rat specific nephrotoxicity: evaluation of the association between d-limonene and alpha2u-globulun. Toxicol. Appl. Pharmacol. 1989. 99:250-259.
12. American Pharmacists Association CEO Blog. Know Your Pharmacist, Know Your Medicine. 2012. Available at: http://www.pharmacist.com/know-your-pharmacist-know-your-medicine. Last Accessed February 21, 2017.

13. National Institute of Health. US National Library of Medicines. Genetics Home Reference. G6PD Gene. Available at https://ghr.nlm.nih.gov/gene/G6PD#conditions. Last Accessed February 22, 2017.

QUESTION 40

1. Schmiedlin-Ren P, Edwards DJ, Fitzsimmons ME, et al. Mechanisms of enhanced oral availability of CYP3A4 substrates by grapefruit constituents. Decreased enterocyte CYP3A4 concentration and mechanism-based inactivation by furanocoumarins. Drug Metab Dispos. 1997 Nov;25(11):1228-33.
2. Bailey DG, Dresser GK, Bend JR. Bergamottin, lime juice, and red wine as inhibitors of cytochrome P450 3A4 activity: comparison with grapefruit juice. Clin Pharmacol Ther. 2003 Jun;73(6):529-37.
3. Li P, Callery PS, Gan LS, Balani SK. Esterase inhibition attribute of grapefruit juice leading to a new drug interaction. Drug Metab Dispos. 2007 Jul;35(7):1023-31. Epub 2007 Mar 28.
4. Tisserand R and Young R. Essential Oil Safety. 2nd ed. Churchill Livingston Elsevier. 2014
5. Wangensteen H, Molden E, Christensen H, Malterud KE.Identification of epoxybergamottin as a CYP3A4 inhibitor in grapefruit peel. Eur J Clin Pharmacol. 2003 Feb;58(10):663-8. Epub 2003 Jan 30.
6. Ho PC, Saville DJ, Wanwimolruk S. Inhibition of human CYP3A4 activity by grapefruit flavonoids, furanocoumarins and related compounds. J Pharm Pharm Sci. 2001 Sep-Dec;4(3):217-27.

QUESTION 41

1. Koch-Weser J, Sellers EM. Drug interaction with coumarin anticoagulants (First of two parts). N Eng J Med 1971;285 : 487-98.
2. Yip ASB, Chow WH, Tai IT, Cheung KL. Adverse effect of topical methylsalicylate ointment on warfarin anticoagulation: an unrecognised potential hazard. Postgrad Med J 1990;66 : 367-9.
3. Tisserand R and Young R. Essential Oil Safety. 2nd ed. Churchill Livingston Elsevier. 2014
4. Buckle J. Clinical Aromatherapy: Essential Oils in Practice. 2nd ed. Churchill Livingstone. 2003.
5. University of California San Diego Anticoagulation Clinic. Your Guide to Anticoagulant Therapy. Available at: https://health.ucsd.edu/specialties/anticoagulation/patients/Documents/Education%20materials%20provided%20in%20new%20patient%20class.pdf. Last Accessed February 21, 2017.

QUESTION 42

1. Heger-Mahn D, Pabst G, Dienel A, Schläfke S, Klipping C. No interacting influence of lavender oil preparation silexan on oral contraception using an ethinyl estradiol/levonorgestrel combination. Drugs R D. 2014 Dec;14(4):265-72. doi: 10.1007/s40268-014-0065-5.
2. Tisserand R and Young R. Essential Oil Safety. 2014. 2nd ed. Churchill Livingstone Elsevier.
3. Buckle J. Clinical Aromatherapy: Essential Oils in Practice. 2nd ed. Churchill Livingstone. 2003.
4. Mayo Clinic. Male condoms. Available at: http://www.mayoclinic.org/tests-procedures/condoms/basics/definition/prc-20014118. Last Accessed February 21, 2017.
5. Office of Women's Health. Birth Control Methods. Available at: https://www.womenshealth.gov/a-z-topics/birth-control-methods. Last Accessed February 21, 2017.
6. Emergency contraception as a backup method. United Nations Population Information Network. Available at: http://www.un.org/popin/popis/journals/network/network172/ec172.html. Last Accessed February 21, 2017.
7. Medicines and Healthcare Products Regulatory Agency, United Kingdom Government. St John's wort: interaction with hormonal contraceptives, including implants. Available at: https://www.gov.uk/drug-safety-update/st-john-s-wort-interaction-with-hormonal-contraceptives-including-implants. Last Accessed February 21, 2017.

QUESTION 43

1. Laino C. Drug Tests Often Trigger False Positives. Available at: http://www.webmd.com/drug-medication/news/20100528/drug-tests-often-trigger-false-positives#1. Last Accessed February 21, 2017.
2. Anderson L (reviewer). Can a Drug Test Lead to a False Positive? Available at: https://www.drugs.com/article/false-positive-drug-tests.html. Last Accessed: February 21, 2017.
3. Brahm, Nancy C., et al. Clinical Consultation. Commonly prescribed medications and potential false-positive urine drug screens. American Journal of Health-System Pharmacy 67.16 (2010).

QUESTION 44

1. Papvassilou MJ. Sur deux cas d'intoxication par la sabine la permèabilité placentaire a l'essence de sabine. Société de Médecine Légale. 1937(15)778-81.

2. Macht D. The action of so-called emmenagogue oils on the isolated uterine strip. J Pharm Exp Ther. 1913(4) 547-53
3. Patoir A et al. Acrtion toxique de l'essence de sabine et de l'armoise sur l'organisme. Comptes Rendues Société Biologique. 1938(127)1326-7
4. Patoir A, Patoir G, Bédrine H, Note sur l'action de l'essence de rue sur l'organisme animal. Comptes Rendues Société Biologique. 1938(127)1324-5
5. Anon. Oil of rue: proposed affirmation of GRAS status with specific limitations as direct human food ingredient. Fed. Regist. 1974(39)34215.
6. Committee for Veterinary Food Products. Rura graveolens, summary report. The European Agency for the Evaluation of Medicinal Products. 1999.
7. Cignada C and Laborde A. Herbal infusions used for induced abortion. J Toxicol 2003(41)235-9
8. Farnsworth NR, Bingel AS, Cordell GA et al. Potential value of plants as sources of new antifertility agents. I J Pharm Sci. 1975(64)535-98
9. DeSmet PAGM, Keller K, Hansel R, Chandler RF. Adverse Effects of Herbal Drugs. Mashhad: Ferdowsi University Press; 1998. p. 235.

QUESTION 45

1. 2014 Annual Report of the American Association of Poison Control Centers' National Poison Data System (NPDS): 32nd Annual Report. Available at: https://aapcc.s3.amazonaws.com/pdfs/annual_reports/2014_AAPCC_NPDS_Annual_Report.pdf. Last Accessed February 23, 2017
2. Tisserand R and Young R. Essential Oil Safety. 2014. 2nd ed. Churchill Livingstone Elsevier.
3. Dotinga R. Poisoned by Essential Oils. Available at: http://www.webmd.com/children/news/20160513/more-children-accidently-poisoned-by-essential-oils. Last Accessed February 23, 2017.
4. Gardiner P. Peppermint (Mentha piperita). Available at: http://www.longwoodherbal.org/peppermint/peppermint.pdf. Last Accessed February 23, 2017.
5. Most Commonly Used Essential Oils. http://naha.org/index.php/explore-aromatherapy/about-aromatherapy/most-commonly-used-essential-oils/. Last Accessed February 23, 2017

QUESTION 46

1. Henley DV, Lipson N, Korach KS, Bloch CA. Prepubertal gynecomastia linked to lavender and tea tree oils. N Engl J Med. 2007 Feb 1;356(5):479-85.
2. Carson CF, Tisserand R, Larkman T. Lack of evidence that essential oils affect puberty. Reprod Toxicol. 2014 Apr;44:50-1. Epub 2014 Feb 17.
3. Kemper KJ, Romm AJ, Gardiner P. Prepubertal gynecomastia linked to lavender and tea tree oils. N Engl J Med. 2007 Jun 14;356(24):2541-2; author reply 2543-4.
4. Dean CJ. Prepubertal gynecomastia linked to lavender and tea tree oils. N Engl J Med. 2007 Jun 14;356(24):2543; author reply 2543-4.
5. Kurtz JL. Prepubertal gynecomastia linked to lavender and tea tree oils. N Engl J Med. 2007 Jun 14;356(24):2542-3; author reply 2543-4.
6. Kalyan S. Prepubertal gynecomastia linked to lavender and tea tree oils. N Engl J Med. 2007 Jun 14;356(24):2542; author reply 2543-4.

QUESTION 48

1. Crawford, G. H., Sciacca, J. R., and James, W. D. Tea tree oil: cutaneous effects of the extracted oil of Melaleuca alternifolia. Dermatitis 2004;15(2):59-66.
2. Del Beccaro MA. Melaleuca oil poisoning in a 17-month-old. Vet Hum Toxicol
3. Jacobs MR, Hornfeldt CS. Melaleuca oil poisoning. J Toxicol Clin Toxicol 1994;32:461-4.
4. Morris MC, Donoghue A, Markowitz JA, Osterhoudt KC. Ingestion of tea tree oil (Melaleuca oil) by a 4-year-old boy. Pediatr Emerg Care 2003;19:169-71.
5. Tisserand, R and Rodney Young. Essential Oil Safety: A Guide for Health Care Professionals. 2nd ed. 2013. Churchill-Livingstone.
6. Seawright A. Comment: Tea tree oil poisoning. Med.J Aust 1993;159:830-831.

QUESTION 49

1. Stewart D. The Chemistry of Essential Oils Made Simple. 4th ed. 2013. Care Publications.
2. Tisserand, R and Rodney Young. Essential Oil Safety: A Guide for Health Care Professionals. 2nd ed. 2014. Churchill-Livingstone.
3. Paul M, Briining G, Bergmann J, Jauch J. Boswellia serrata, Boswellia papyrifera and Boswellia carterii, respectively, Boswellia

sacra Phytochem Anal. 2012 Mar-Apr; 23 (2): 184-9. Doi: 10.1002 / pca.1311. Epub 2011 Aug 20.

4. Moussaieff A, Rimmerman N, Bregman T , Straiker A , Fields CC , et al. Incensole acetate, an incense component, elicits psychoactivity by activating TRPV3 channels in the brain. FASEB J. 2008 Aug. 22 (8): 3024-34. Doi: 10.1096 / fj.07-101865. Epub 2008 May 20.

5. Woolley CL, Suhail MM, Smith BL, Boren KE, et al. Chemical differentiation of Boswellia sacra and Boswellia carterii essential oils by gas chromatography and chiral gas chromatography-mass spectrometry. J Chromatogr A. 2012 Oct 26;1261:158-63. doi: 10.1016/j.chroma.2012.06.073. Epub 2012 Jun 28.

QUESTION 50

1. Lis-Balchin, M. and S. Hart, 1999. Studies on the mode of action of the essential oil of lavender (*Lavandula angustifolia* P. Miller). Phytother. Res., 13: 540–542

2. Lis-Balchin, M.T. and S.G. Deans, 1997. Bioactivity of selected plant essential oil against Listeria monocytogenes. J. Appl. Microbiol., 82: 759–762

3. Jianu C, Pop G, Gruia AT and Horhat FG. Composition and Antimicrobial Activity of Lavender and Lavandin Essential Oils / Int. J. Agric. Biol., Vol. 15, No. 4, 2013

4. Weir's Lane Lavender. Lavender v. Lavandin ... what's the difference? Available at: https://www.weirslanelavender.ca/pages/lavender-v-lavandin-whats-the-difference. Last Accessed February 23, 2017.

MORE ESSENTIALS QUESTION 2

1. Pitchford, Paul. Healing with Whole Foods: Oriental Traditions and Modern Nutrition. Berkeley, Calif: North Atlantic Books, 1996.

MORE ESSENTIALS QUESTION 3

1. Methylsulfonylmethane (MSM). Monograph. Altern Med Rev. 2003 Nov;8(4):438-41.http://www.altmedrev.com/publications/8/4/438.pdf. Last Accessed February 23, 2017.

2. Morton JI, Siegel BV. Effects of oral dimethyl sulfoxide and dimethyl sulfone on murine autoimmune lymphoproliferative disease. Proc Soc Exp Biol Med 1986:183:227-230.

3. Barrager E, Veltmann JR Jr, Schauss AG, Schiller RN. A multicentered, open-label trial on the safety and efficacy of methylsulfonyl-methane in the treatment of seasonal allergic rhinitis. J Altern Complement Med 2002;8:167-17

ACKNOWLEDGEMENTS

Thank you to the staff of designers, editors and managers at Growing Healthy Homes who helped me bring this book to you.

Thank you to Catey Hall for introducing me to the transformative power to essential oils, to Crystal Burchfield for a million layers of support, and to Jared Turner for empowering every dream and weathering every storm.

BIOGRAPHY

Dr. Lindsey Elmore is a small-town girl with a big dream. She is a speaker, wellness advocate, and now an author. What Lindsey does well is analyze data to inform her presentations, and take complicated science information and make it simple. Originally trained as a chemist and then a clinical pharmacist, she now crafts memorable, relatable science stories about essential oils, herbs, and foods.

She obtained an undergraduate degree in chemistry from the University of Alabama Birmingham and a doctorate in pharmacy from the University of California San Francisco. She completed her first-year post-doctoral residency in pharmacy practice at Princeton Baptist Medical Center in Birmingham, AL and her second-year specialty residency in ambulatory care at New Hanover Regional Medical Center in Wilmington, NC. She is a Board-Certified Pharmacotherapy Specialist, and licensed to practice in three US states. She believes that the pharmacist is healthcare's most underutilized resource. Not only do pharmacists know medicines, they are teaching patients how to optimize their medicines (if your pharmacist misses either of these traits, break away from the chain and go to support a local, independent pharmacy). Please vote for leaders who support expansion of pharmacy practice acts; as has been demonstrated in North Carolina, pharmacists improve disease state control and save health care dollars when they are granted authority to manage medication.

Dr. Elmore has spoken on five continents to local, state, national and international audiences. Her presentation materials have been translated into more than 20 languages. She is published in a wide variety of pharmacy and medical journals, and has a long history of service with the American Society of Health System Pharmacists. She served as a visiting scholar at the University of Zambia, Department of Medicine and provided direct patient care in family medicine, community pharmacy, and inpatient care for years before changing course to embrace health care instead of sick care.

Dr. Elmore is passionate about mindful wellness. She is a Certified Aroma Yoga® Instructor, and an advocate of whole foods as medicine. She has been a patient of Chinese medicine and acupuncture for over a decade, and blends Eastern and Western concepts of health in all her teaching.

Dr. Elmore is The Farmacist online, and her teaching has inspired hundreds of thousands of people to take ownership of their health and wellness, and it grows every day. Join her on her journey: @thefarmacistala on Facebook, Instagram, Twitter, and Snapchat. www.thefarmacistalabama.com to join the mailing list or read the blog.

In her spare time, Dr. Elmore enjoys giving thanks, swimming in oceans, rivers and streams, singing with her partner Benjy, dancing alone in her apartment, and watching her brother play professional baseball. She and Benjy currently reside in New York City.

INDEX

Symbols

1,8-cineole 40, 41, 154, 161, 163, 180, 184, 205, 212, 219, 220, 221, 222, 278

A

Adverse reaction 23
Allergy
  essential oil 46, 48, 139, 140, 160, 248, 262
  nut oil 132, 263
Alpha-pinene 234
Alpha-thujene 234
Anise essential oil 176
Asthma 46, 158, 160, 161, 162, 172, 254, 270, 272
Autoimmune disease 46, 167, 168, 169, 275

B

Basil essential oil 149, 150, 151
Bergepten 176
Breastfeeding 210, 213, 214, 215, 226
Breastmilk 90, 213, 226

C

Cancer 175, 176, 177, 184, 262, 274, 276, 278
Cassia essential oil 24, 29, 78, 94, 104, 114, 146, 198, 252
Cedarwood essential oil 17, 34, 50, 104, 137, 162, 235
Child(ren) 8, 19, 24, 50, 79, 81, 82, 90, 94, 95, 101, 103, 104, 105, 116, 155, 161, 163, 164, 185, 193, 194, 208, 217, 218, 219, 220, 221, 222, 225, 226, 230, 252, 268, 273, 274, 278, 282

Cinnamon essential oil 22, 29, 60, 78, 84, 86, 90, 93, 94, 114, 125, 146, 154, 156, 176, 198, 212, 218, 219, 262, 269
Citral 29, 36, 125, 140, 161, 176, 205, 210, 211, 264, 271
Citrus essential oils 22, 23, 29, 34, 36, 40, 41, 42, 44, 49, 104, 105, 140, 196, 264
Clove essential oil 22, 23, 24, 29, 60, 71, 78, 84, 86, 90, 94, 104, 146, 154, 176, 212, 218, 219, 252, 254, 268
COPD 158, 161, 272

D

Dermatitis 48, 49, 50, 145, 146, 147, 230, 255, 264, 265, 283
Diabetes 126, 153, 154, 155, 156, 169, 172, 268, 269, 275, 277
Distillation 15, 16, 22, 33, 34, 35, 36, 44
Drug interaction 175, 184, 189, 190, 193, 196, 210, 211, 214

E

(E)-anethole 175, 176, 193, 210, 211, 214
Eczema 46, 230
Eucalyptus essential oil 60, 104, 105, 161, 181, 212, 217, 219, 220, 221, 222

F

Fennel essential oil 24, 42, 87, 156, 175, 176, 177, 181, 182, 198, 209, 211, 214, 215, 279

Frankincense essential oil 34, 35, 42, 86, 105, 137, 228, 233, 234, 235

G

Geraniol125, 127, 140, 176, 180, 210, 262, 264
Ginger essential oil 127, 129, 274
Grapefruit essential oil 36, 40, 49, 114, 181, 195, 196, 280

H

Hormones 123, 124, 175, 224
Hypersensitivity 46, 47, 48, 161, 230, 254, 255
Hypertension 179, 180, 181, 182, 201, 268, 269, 277

I

IgE 46, 140, 160, 161
Ingestion 22, 23, 24, 78, 79, 140, 164, 213, 218, 221, 230, 231, 252, 283

J

Jasmine essential oils 35, 40, 146

L

Lavender essential oil 11, 48, 58, 87, 104, 114, 121, 124, 126, 127, 129, 130, 137, 155, 162, 175, 177, 180, 181, 200, 223, 224, 228, 237, 238, 255, 261, 262, 263, 269, 275, 276, 277, 281, 283, 284
Lemongrass essential oils 50, 78, 90, 94, 146, 156, 191, 210
Limonene 41, 159, 160, 163, 182, 193, 234
Lipid Pneumonia 105, 164, 273, 274

M

Menthol 24, 29, 155, 156, 159, 161, 162, 163, 180, 194, 200, 214, 219, 220, 253, 271
Monoterpene 8, 27, 28, 29, 30, 69, 104, 163, 251

N

Nerol 29, 125, 176, 180, 210
Nursing 208, 209, 210, 214
Nutmeg essential oil 22, 156, 193, 213, 269

O

Olfaction 64, 116, 159
Orange essential oil 22, 40, 41, 49, 58, 86, 114, 127, 155, 176, 185, 235, 253, 278
Oregano essential oil 29, 78, 90, 94, 104, 109, 114, 146, 156, 198, 212, 218, 258

P

Para-cymene 234
Pets 91, 103, 104
Phenol 8, 27, 28, 29, 31, 69, 104, 251, 253, 271, 276, 277
Pregnancy 125, 172, 200, 201, 210, 211, 212, 213, 214, 246, 266

R

Rue essential oil 49, 114, 213, 214, 282

S

Sage essential oil 22, 42, 58, 94, 114, 121, 146, 180, 181, 182, 191, 212, 277
Seizure 149, 150, 180, 221
Sesquiterpene 8, 27, 28, 29, 31, 69, 140, 251

Skin sensitivity 50, 82, 146,
147
Smell (see olfaction) 40, 63, 64,
66, 86, 103, 104, 184, 212, 238,
249, 263
Stress 50, 124, 126, 127, 128,
129, 130, 145, 146, 147, 184,
262, 263, 265, 266, 269

T

Tea Tree essential oil 41, 42, 58,
105, 124, 130, 156, 175, 177,
219, 224, 228, 229, 230,
231, 255, 258, 262, 275, 276,
283
Thyroid 124, 126, 127, 151, 154,
261, 265, 268
TRPV receptor 161, 234, 271,
284

V

Vetiver essential oil 137, 235

BRING THE ESSENTIALS TO LIFE!

Dr. Elmore is a sought-after speaker who provides webinars, stage presentations, book readings as well as content and curriculum development.

Her quirky approach, animated movements, and memorable stories make even the most difficult science easy for beginners and experts alike.

To book a class or series of classes based on the content of this book or on any topic related to natural wellness, please email thefarmacistalabama@gmail.com or visit us on the web at www.thefarmacistalabama.com.

To obtain additional copies of this book and for more information on other books by Growing Healthy Homes, please visit our website at www.GrowingHealthyHomes.com